# Neeps & Strae

*by*

**Charlie Allan**

*Illustrations by*
*Rhoda Howie*

**Ardo Publishing Company**
Methlick, Aberdeenshire AB41 7HR

**To Fiona**

*Published by Ardo Publishing Company, Buchan*

Printed in Great Britain by BPCWheaton Ltd, Exeter

# Contents

*Continued over*

# Contents

4

# Acknowledgements

It was once usual to thank one's secretarial staff for their tireless efforts to interpret the author's writing and correct his spelling. Now, as is usual, all I have to thank in that department is my computer, and there I must warn you that some of my machine's American ideas may annoy you if I haven't got them all out.

I am grateful to Rhoda Howie, not only for the quality of her drawings and photography, but for her willingness to work to my demanding timetables without appearing to mind.

Fiona Allan has made her usual pleasing and efficient job of the desk-top publishing... she is the one responsible for how the book looks. Susie Allan scanned the drawings into her computer. And Sarah Purdie read the proofs with the eye of a pedant with a long lens.

A number of my fellow Aberdonians were particularly good sources of ideas and even worked at feeding me lines. I consider that a particularly noble thing to do as it must be tempting to keep them to themselves. They include James and Sandy Fowlie, Bill Ferguson and my relatives Johnny, Sir Maitland and Stephen Mackie, and especially Jimmy Low who, as grieve, terrorised my farm for more than forty years.

And finally, my wife's contribution to these stories was immense. Much of it was made in front of a well stocked fire and catalysed by some of the better malts. Those creative sessions have been among the high points of our marriage which is now well through its fourth decade. Her instinct for what would have happened next or what who would have said, and her suggestions for subjects for stories have been such a help that, had she not been my wife, I would have been in danger from the charge of plagiarism. It is therefore neither as a political gesture nor as a mere expression of affection that I have dedicated this volume to Fiona.

# Foreword

I cannot claim these stories as entirely my own. They have their origins among the folk of the North-east Lowlands of Scotland. Some are little more than expansions of the timeless and often apocryphal stories which are told at the cattle markets and watering holes. And even when they are more truly my own work of fiction, these tales echo the country people, particularly of Buchan and Formartine... their attitudes, repartee, witticisms and observations.

They would never have been written had it not been for Allan Wright, then a fellow-producer at the BBC. He suggested the programme a Poem, a Song and a Story. The poem would be by Tim Douglas, Jean Redpath would sing a song and I would write and read a story. The whole programme was to be fifteen minutes so, as Tim Douglas wrote long poems, the stories had to be short.

Perhaps they are too short. *Puddockstane*, where the husband makes such a hash of selling his lambs that the wife decides she'll have to do it at the next sales, is one of my favourites. It could easily have been the first chapter only. We could have followed the pair as the wife got the whole enterprise on the same solid footing as that upon which she kept the house.

Perhaps *Oceans o' Muck* should have been taken further as the husband's suckler cow business declined and the wife's organic vegetables prospered.

And surely someone will make a whole book of what happens to the white settler when all his dreams of a goodlife fall apart.

At any rate the programme was a success and ran to four series. It made a comeback each Christmas until 1988 and the stories were then broadcast in Farming Today on Radio Four on Monday mornings.

I hope this selection from those stories will give the reader a flavour of the Scottish countryside in the first three quarters of the 20th century.

# CHAPTER ONE

# *Neeps tae Ca'*

GEORDIE THOMSON was a good man and willing. He never questioned the system that gave him a six-day week from six in the morning till six at night, and of course there were the horse to be seen to before breakfast and after supper. He would never have complained when, at busy times like harvest, he had to work even longer hours. There were no holidays ever and yet Geordie Thomson did what he was told and did it well. But there was one part of farm work that he just could not stand and that was ca'in neeps. And on a stock farm in Aberdeenshire, in the days before the neep pu'er made it possible to load turnips from the comfort of your heated, quiet safety cab, a horseman who didn't like working with frozen neeps could have a pretty miserable life. You see there was very little silage before the 1950s and Buchan was never a very good place for making hay, so the stock had to eat a prodigious number of turnips between the November and May terms.

Geordie knew Little Ardo was a dairy farm with forty milking cows and that we kept all the followers so, when he arrived on the 29th of November for his six-month contract, he was looking forward with little relish to his winter.

He wouldn't have taken a job on a stock farm of any kind but it was 1933. That was the worst year of the Depression when practically every farm in Aberdeenshire decided to make do with one man fewer. One of the other lads he'd been fee'd with at his

7

last place had been among the dozens who took refuge in Inverurie Town Hall at the term because they not only lost their jobs but their tied houses as well. So Geordie had been relieved to accept the half-crown in arles to assure his livelihood even if the bargain only entitled him to another £27.17s 6d. for what he realised full well would be a hard six months.

Mind you, the new third horseman was well enough pleased with the promise of his first day as he waited in the stable for his orders at six o'clock. It was raining so at least there would be no ca'in neeps. He'd heard that the grieve was a gie hardy devil but at least there would be an inside job for Geordie that day.

But there was no such luck. When the grieve came out on the stroke of six, the foreman was put to the plough, the second to Kelly sawmill for sticks, "Aye, and you, Thomson, you'll ken whar the neep park is, you'll ca' neeps." So ca' neeps he did, all day in the rain.

By the next morning the rain had turned to sleet. At least there would be no neeps today. The land would be far too wet for the horse to work on it and no grieve on earth would put men out in weather like that.

Well now, if Geordie Thomson had had a surprise the day before, he was absolutely dumbfounded at yoking time on his second day at Little Ardo, for it's a good draining farm and it takes a fair sup rain to make it unworkable. The first two pairs were put to the plough and Geordie was sent back to the neep park; "Aye, and Geordie, ye'll ken the workins o' the place better the day so we'll expect an extra load or twa."

Geordie Thomson wondered at this place he had landed at; oh aye, he would fairly have stayed at Waterside if only he'd been spiered - though he knew it had been a bare enough hole.

All day long Geordie worked away bringing home the turnips. He was soon soaked but by afternoon the day had turned harder until the sleet turned to snow and the frost set in. By the time he got home, the third horseman's jacket would have stood up by itself at the fire to dry.

When Geordie saw the dawning of his third day at Little Ardo he was quite certain that there would be a change at last. The

8

overnight frost had set the earth like concrete. There was a fair covering of snow which was just offering to blow and set up little drifts along the back road. Not even this grieve would expect his men to go out in weather like that, especially with the neep shed full and a fair heap in the close.

When the tramp of the grieve's tackety boots came crunching across the close it was like the march of doom.

"Aye lads, it's far too hard for the ploo the day and I can see there could be a storm coming so we'll need plenty of neeps in.

The three o' ye a' awa and ca' neeps."

Geordie thought the end of the world had come, and after a couple of hours in the neep park he could well have done with a bit of hell fire, if only to warm him up. The neeps had been pu'd the day before by the orraman and, to give him his due, the grieve. There they lay all neatly topped and tailed and set in neat rows. But the overnight frost had frozen them, the sleet stuck them together and the day's snow had covered them with a sort of nightmare topping.

The turnips had to be unwillingly ripped from the frozen ground by fingers that started cold and grew worse. And Geordie knew the rules. Each man had to keep six neeps moving at once for as each pair landed in the cart, he must have two more sailing through the air and another two in his hands ready for the throw. The rhythm of the work and the need to keep up with the foreman did eventually get the circulation going, and, while Geordie was miserable, at least by dinner time he had conquered the cold.

Now Little Ardo farm stands on a small hill overlooking the village of Methlick. It is very heaven on a fine day with grand views up the Ythan valley to the Braes o' Gight, across the river to Formartine and down stream to Newburgh and the sea. But on a winter's day the wind can come at you from any direction without interruption.

And so it happened on Geordie Thomson's fourth day on the place. The wind was in the North and there is no shelter between Methlick and the Arctic. The snow was falling horizontally. It would have been on a day like that that Napoleon decided that if the Russians wanted their country that bad, he would head back to Paris. Surely there would be no neeps on a day like that - but then again - he'd already been wrong three times and this grieve was no mere Napoleon.

They didn't even hear the grieve tramping over the close at six. The first they knew of him was when he burst into the stable in a white swirl of snow, and it took two of them to bar the door against the gale.

"Aye lads," said the grieve, wiping the snow off his arms, "it's far too coorse to put the horse out the day. Ye'll just need to get your tapners and ging out tae the park yersels and pu' some neeps for Thomson tae tak in i' the mornin."

CHAPTER TWO

# A Trip to the Circus

THIS IS about the time of year when my great grandfather took
sixty-four bairns from Auchnagatt to the great Barnum and
Bailly's circus in Aberdeen. In 1890 a trip from Auchnagatt to
Aberdeen was a safari of some magnitude, even after the coming
of the railway. It was nearly thirty miles away and taking the
entire Sunday school, as my great grandfather intended, was
considered an act of daring to the point of foolhardiness. "You're
bound to lose some of them, John Mackie. And how'll you feed
them? And what if you miss the train and you'll never keep track
o' them aa?"

"I'll easy keep track o' them, never you fear," said John
Mackie. "I'll coont them onto the train and I'll coont them aff at
Aiberdeen and I'll coont them intil the circus and I'll coont them
back ontil the train and *you* can coont them when we get back to
Auchnagatt."

The cost of the great day would be no less than four shillings
a head, despite the old man's efforts in getting a discount from
Messrs Barnum and Bailly for being five dozen strong and the
excursion rate on the train. Now four shillings might not seem a
great deal today but to the cottar families of Buchan in the 1890s,
with their high fertility and their low wages, that was a large sum.

But there had been a small surplus on the Arnage Games,
which was run in aid of the Hall fund, and my great grandfather
arranged that funds be made available from that, so that a charge

11

of only one shilling per child would have to be made. Mind you that was still too much for some. In those cases private arrangements were made. No child was to be left behind... on the way there, at least.

The great day came. Every child between the ages of five and thirteen in the Parish of Auchnagatt assembled in front of the Baron's Hotel. They were in their Sunday best which in many cases was not that good, but they were clean, cropped and eager. They were brought by their parents, some of whom actually wept for this would be the first time that there'd been as much as thirty miles between them and their bairns. And there were those who said they were quite right to weep for John Mackie would never manage to bring them all home again. Six children to each of six gigs and the rest in a phaeton, the gallant sixty-four set off to a breathless cheer and bumped and swayed along the six miles to Arnage station.

There John Mackie duly counted the sixty-four bairns onto the train, ten to a compartment and the fourteen littlest ones in the compartment with him. And each with a bottle of Mrs Mackie's hairst ale and a quarter of breid.

The train took off for the town to a another cheer. Excitement was high. Few of the children had been in a train before and some hadn't been out of the parish. The youth of Auchnagatt was experiencing an expansion of their world that was sudden and great.

When they reached the first station John Mackie jumped out to run along the platform for another count of his charges. He was met by his first crisis. What with the excitement and Mrs Mackie's hairst ale, and there being no corridors on the train, and no facilities, half the children were needin and a few were *affa* needin.

"Oh my god!" He hadn't thought of this one. If he let some of them out, how would he get them counted back into their tens? There'd be little doubt there would be just as many more needin when he got to Logierieve. And he'd have the whole performance to go through again at Udny.

There was only one thing for it. He got the whole lot out at

Ellon, needin or no.

Now the facilities at Ellon were hardly made for sixty-four at a time. But country bairns in those days were resourceful and John Mackie soon had them counted back into their compartments. After only a short delay, the guard waved his green flag and blew his whistle and, to the obvious relief of the station master, the train moved out.

At Kittybrewster station the gallant sixty-four were counted out and herded the half mile to the great marquee in Central Park.

Remember these were not modern children, totally spoiled by electronics. There is nothing you could take a modern class from Auchnagatt to Aberdeen to see that would astonish them. They have seen it all before on the telly. And indeed, no matter what it is, they will have seen the best on the telly. And worse than that the telly cheats: they only show you the best bits and if anyone does anything wrong, they do it again.

But to those country children before the First World War, everything was astonishing. The town, the big top, clowns, the brassey band and elephants were quite new images. When the lion tamer entered the cage, the country bairns fully expected him to have fo fight or flee. When the clowns threw gallons of paint at one another, these bairns were not reminded of Noel's House Party. They weren't reminded of anything. It was all astonishing. One little boy when he got home said to his mother "and Mam, there wis a pooler bear" which must have been an exaggeration, surely.

After the show they were counted out of the marquee and counted into the Kittybrewster tearoom for their tea: white fish followed by a piece, and jam and cakes.

There were many crises when someone got lost, or hid or stole somebody else's piece, but after umpteen such, the bairns were marched back to Kittybrewster station and eventually the train carrying the bairns pulled, with a sigh of relief, back into Arnage station. The convoy of gig and the phaeton carried them back to Auchnagatt where the anxious parents were waiting. Would Mr Mackie have brought them all safely home? There were others who had warned against so foolish an adventure who were actually hoping that at least one or even two children would have been left behind.

But as the convoy wound down the brae from Arnage the counting started. There seemed to be plenty of bairns. "My god! There's sixty-five."

"Oh! John Mackie's fairly deen it noo."

Consternation reigned. What would Auchnagatt do with an extra bairn? But when the convoy arrived and the anxious parents had claimed their sixty-four bairns, there wasn't one left over. Each had got a home.

It was quite a mystery and John Mackie waited years before telling the village that the extra bairn had been in the town at the dentist and had arranged to meet the party at the circus and get home with them.

# CHAPTER THREE

# *Willie Gerrie of Puddockstane*

PUDDOCKSTANE WAS too far up the hill to be a good farm. It sat on the north side of the valley and looked down on the bright red earth below where, even in 1952, farmers could grow ten quarters of barley in a good year. Willie Gerrie could only grow oats and he had to tell lies to get his yields up to so much as six quarters. He liked to grow some nevertheless, for the look of the thing, though there's little doubt life would have been a lot easier for Willie if he had bought his grain and his straw. It would have saved him the anguish of watching the fat cats below, harvesting in August and September, and the embarrassment of seeing them looking up at his frost-covered stooks in November.

Puddockstane ran to 300 acres of hill and 50 of in-bye on which Willie grew his oats, a few turnips and a suppie hay to get his stock through the winter, which was just about a month longer than on the carse land below. That meant a long time's feeding for the 200 Blackfaces and for the two Shorthorn cross Ayrshire cows which provided a calf for sale and milk for the house. Mrs Gerrie kept hens (White Wyndots). They were grand layers and with eggs going as high as seven shillings a dozen, there were times when the lady of the house was bringing in as much from her 50 hens and the odd kebbuk she made with the surplus milk, as Willie made from the rest of the farm. But that was no surprise

15

really, for she was one of those gifted few who can do whatever's asked of them and do it well, and who are content with what they've got whatever that may be. Annie Gerrie was once asked what she thought heaven would be like and her answer was typical: "I aye think heaven will jist be like Puddockstane on a fine day."

Mind you, fine days weren't that common at Puddockstane and that fact didn't escape Willie. For while Mrs Gerrie got heaven on earth every now and again, life for Willie always seemed hellish. His rickles of stone dykes were neither enough to keep the sheep in, nor the deer out, in winter. The grass was always slow to come and quick to go. And he always seemed to get a bad draw at the lamb sales: his were always sold first before the bidding got going, or just after the main buyers' floats were full. Still, the farmer of Puddockstane stuck at it and we should admire him for that.

Now it would be wrong to say Willie Gerrie had a weakness for strong drink; he hadn't. But at the same time he didn't have a strong head for the stuff and very little tended to cloud his judgement. And that was what happened when he bought the top price ram at the wee ram sale that followed the first sale of store lambs at Strathbeegle.

Willie's lambs should never have been at the sale - his place was just too late to have lambs ready for the first sale, but pride would send some - and pride got his usual fall. His lambs 'stolen' once again, Willie got a willing ear in the bar as he poured in the drams and poured out his complaints about his luck, the state of things, the tax (though in truth he never paid any) and the terrible job the government was making.

It was good crack and Willie began to enjoy himself fine. But the drams, while they fairly dulled the pain of the poor prices he'd been bid for his lambs, didn't do a great deal for Willie's judgement - and that wasn't his strong suit at the best of times. So when Jimmy Gow, the sheep dealer, came up with a solution to Puddockstane's problems, Willie didn't even have enough wit left to be on his guard.

"What you need is a right good new tup, to give you a bigger

16

lamb to catch the top of the trade."

Now there was some truth in that for Willie had always raked around for a bargain in the butcher's pen and the most he'd ever paid for a tup was short of £20. Right enough, that was it, he'd just go and buy the best ram in the sale and that would do the trick.

There was time before the rams were sold for a few more drams to raise Willie's expectations, and reduce his judgement still further. And in that time Jimmy Gow was able to persuade our man that he had just the tup for the job. It was fabulously bred and if it was maybe not the biggest tup in the sale, that was because the dealer had been a wee bit short of feed in the spring. But what a bonny head he had and plenty bone about him - what potential!

By the time it came to the sale, it was just a question of how much they would make poor Willie pay.

"Two hunner poun'? A hunner then? Fifty?"

"Yes" roared Willie and the auctioneer was off, taking bids five pounds at a time. No-one actually saw anyone else bidding. Just Willie - but you could fairly see Willie was keen. When the bidding was at £60, the auctioneer could see he was good for another tenner. And the gleam in his eye gave away the game that, at £100, he would easily go to £110. So the question of who else was bidding was purely academic. One bidder who is keen is fully as good as two to the skilled auctioneer.

And so it was that Willie paid £200 for that ram - twice the next highest that day - and despite having given him such a bargain, the seller still gave a luck penny of 10 shillings. Oh yes, he was all heart that Jimmy Gow.

The forty Puddockstane lambs not having made enough even to pay for his purchase, the farmer set off for home in his old Fergie tractor with his battered float trailing behind.

The seeds of doubt germinated and sprouted on the road home, and when the grey lady turned into the close at Puddockstane they were ready for a bitter harvest.

"How did you get on? Where's your cheque for the lambs?" said Annie, trying to show keen but fearing the worst - or not quite the worst for the truth was far worse than Annie feared. "Nae cheque? How much did you pay for that lamb? He's nae a lamb - he's a shearling? Oh my God, WILLIE!"

No more was said though. Willie got a pen for his ram, unhitched the float, put past the tractor, fed the kye and came and took his tea in silence. Nothing was said in the short evening.

Willie was first in bed and turned his face sadly to the wall. When Annie came in beside him, she sat up for a while and then said:

"Aye Willie, I think I should maybe take the next draft of lambs to the mart."

"Aye, I think maybe you should."

Annie sighed and pulled up the covers. Her warm hand touched him on the shoulder. "And I bet next year we've some right good lambs off that fine tup you bought."

Willie Gerrie's hand sought the hand on his shoulder. "Thanks lass," he said.

## CHAPTER FOUR

# *The Doctors*

GRAHAM AND Willie were the sons of the grieve and the baillie at the fine farm of Drumilton in Aberdeenshire. They were loons in the late 1940s when the horrors of war were still fresh enough in the minds to keep the hearts determined and optimistic about the new world that was to be built out of the holocaust.

But that was all for adults. The problems and pleasures of the two small boys were simple and short term, but intense. They dug for arnuts on the broom hillie, chased the doos in the old barn until they dropped and could be killed for the pot, played at housies and fought interminably over their lames - the bits of broken china that were such a source of pride and passion in the domestic fantasies of the young. Their biggest frustration was that they were too young to go to the Wolf Cubs with the big boys.

The two were far from being a matching set. They were thrown together by the fact that they were the only boys of six and seven at Drumilton at the time. Graham was a beautiful child with a shock of red hair and yet hardly any freckles and if he couldn't sing, the birds would come down from the trees just to see his smile. When the quines played that skipping game where they sang:

> *She is handsome she is pretty,*
> *She is the girl from the Golden City.*
> *She has lovers one-two-three.*
> *Pray now tell me who they be.*

19

You could always be sure of one of them:
*Graham Marshall is his name.*

But the girls hardly ever chose Willie; he was plainer alto-gether. Shorter and rounder than his pal, he had that lifeless non-descript hair that was best suited to the universal hairstyle of the time - the close crop with a tuft sticking out the front.

I am sure it was just one of those unkindnesses which are so characteristic of the rural North-east of Scotland, but it is said that Willie's plainness was first pointed up, unwittingly, by the Rev-erend Ian McGregor.

Willie was born in a particularly fertile week, and the new doctor was very keen on getting the ladies into the cottage hospital for their confinements, so there was quite a line-up of new parishioners for the minister to view. He worked his way down the line, heaping praise on the beauty of each babe in turn, until he came to the child who was going to become Willie. Now, Mr McGregor was an honest man and yet a kindly one and that, you will see immediately, is an unfortunate combination of virtues to bring to the task of viewing the newly born.

Eventually, after some frantic searching, Mr McGregor turned to Willie's mother and offered her, "He'll look well in the kilt."

But Willie was a clever boy and made up, to some extent, for his lack of physical charm by his animated conversation. When you are only six you haven't got a lot of experience upon which to draw for stories but that didn't stop Willie, for he had a wonderful imagination.

So I guess you've got the picture.

The boys had an idyllic life until Willie had to go to hospital to have his appendix out. The poor lad was 'affa feart' and told his mother that there was no need for the hospital. She would just kiss it, like she had done when he had skinned his knees, and it would be all better in the morning. It was no use. Into hospital he went.

All turned out well of course and Willie was soon showing off his scars to Graham who was duly impressed. But what impressed Graham most was Willie's description of the enema he'd been given before his operation. It had been 'affa sair', and the more impressed Graham was, the the more Willie coloured the story up. At every telling that enema got to be a more and more horrendous event. "But what was in't?" Graham wanted to know. Gradually it came to include all the nippy things that Willie could think of: mustard, vinegar and pepper.

Willie had been home for a fortnight and had more or less recovered. The grieve's wife, Graham's mother, was cooking. It was when she was setting the table that she noticed that the mustard jar was empty. That was funny - she could have sworn there was quite a bit left. She would just have to make some more. But, by what she thought was an odd coincidence, the vinegar bottle was empty as well. Oh dear! it just wasn't her day, for she'd already made an extra trip to the shop because she had run out of pepper. "Oh really, I couldn't organise a booze-up in the Naafi with a ten bob note," she said to herself.

Just at that moment all hell broke out in the steading: screeching and shrieking that would have wakened the dead. She dropped her cooking and went to see what those two boys were doing next and tell them to stop it.

She ran towards the piggery from where the noise was coming, to be met by a demented little pig, bolting into the distance and squealing as only a pig can. And there were the two boys in wide-eyed amazement, Willie with an oilcan in his hand from which a foul-looking, mustard-coloured substance trickled.

"I tell't ye it was sair," said Willie to Graham.

*That story appeared in Leopard Magazine where it was recognised by cartoonist Sandy Cheyne as being based on an incident in his childhood. That was no wonder. It was given me by his former wife Lindy Cheyne.*

# CHAPTER FIVE

# *The Athlete*

THERE'S A lot of talk these days about the conflict in the countryside between farmers on the one hand and wildlife on the other. You'd never think it to listen to the argument, but in the part of Scotland I know best the wildlife is winning, or perhaps I should say, staging a recovery. Certainly wildlife is far more plentiful in East Aberdeenshire than when I was a boy. I never saw a fox as a child and deer were so scarce that I clearly remember the time I did see one of them. I was fifty-six when I saw my first badger. And birds, my goodness, we've even got an osprey now and perhaps even a fish eagle. There are problems of course. I haven't heard a corncraik for years, but I believe that the main enemy of wildlife nowadays isn't farmers but drivers. There are far more drivers on the roads now and they're going ever faster. But, while there is more wildlife about, it's still going at the same speed, and the poor old hedgehog still thinks his prickles will protect him from a four litre Jaguar doing a hundred miles per hour. One's sympathies in all this carnage on the roads must lie with the animals of course, but it has to be recognised that a bang from a fox or a roe deer can make quite a mess of one of these flimsy new cars. And now there's a new threat to the motorist. A much larger though slower-moving animal has started to roam our country roads and it has the potential to cause all kinds of damage. I refer, of course, to the jogger (sometimes called the marathon runner - though not by those real marathon runners who are athletes and consider themselves much better than joggers).

Now you will recognise immediately that it's not the farmers or trades-people of rural Scotland who have taken up this extraordinary pastime. It's the incomers. In Aberdeenshire it's the oilies who've come to live in the countryside and work in the towns of Aberdeen and Peterhead. After a hard day on the telephone and drinking endless cups of coffee, they like to work off the considerable effects of their business lunches by peching round a few miles of country road in their fancy tracksuits. And it's hardly safe, you know. Farmers in that part of the world have developed a style of driving which doesn't involve looking at the road - that's so they can concentrate on their neighbours' crops as they drive along - and, while there have been no fatalities yet, there have been some narrow squeaks as slow moving oilmen jump for safety from fast moving cars driven by farmers.

The locals think nothing of this jogging. They shake their heads, move their pipes to the other sides of their mouths and say: "They must have awful little to do." And it was that sort of contempt for the oilies and their jogging that got Sandy Strachan into that spot of bother.

To cut a long story short, Sandy had had a pint too many when he got into an argument with some of the joggers in Mike's bar. Sandy was trying to put the view that agriculture was the only real industry in the country and, at any rate, far more important than dookin for oil in the North Sea. He got more and more frustrated as the drink made his point of view more and more obvious to himself and his putting of it more and more amusing to the oilies. At last, close to tears of frustration, he closed the discussion, in the time-honoured way, with a string of abuse. Now that would have been alright had his invective not finished with a scathing attack on the oilies' prowess as joggers: "Onybody could dae better - crawlin roon the roads." The inevitable happened and Sandy ended up taking wagers running well into three figures that he could run the Aberdeen Marathon Race - all 26 miles of it.

Now Sandy Strachan might not have been a giant when it

23

came to intellectual discussion but he was a good farmer and had been a good centre half in the school football team. But that had been thirty years ago. Nowadays he never ran and only walked when he absolutely had to. He drove a Range-Rover everywhere, even through his fields to check the stock. And for most of those thirty years Sandy had never denied himself anything in the way of food or drink if he wanted it... and those he usually did. As a result you could hardly imagine a less likely candidate for running for a bus let alone a marathon.

In Mike's bar, that fateful night, it was pointed out that a marathon runner runs the first eight miles on the excitement of the occasion, the second on his fitness and that the last ten miles was a matter of pure guts. "Oh well," said Gibby the Postie, "You'll be a' right for the last ten, Sandy, for you've the biggest guts in Methlick." But, true as that was, Sandy Strachan, 19 stones and still growing, started training for the Aberdeen Marathon the very next day. He looked out the old football shorts but a look was enough. He wouldn't even get one leg in there. Then he had another idea. It would be better to wear ordinary clothes at first. Then if anyone came along he could pretend he was just out for a walk. That worked quite well. Sandy left the Range-Rover in the garage and trotted round the stock each morning and each evening. And if you're 19 stones and doing that twice a day you're too tired to go to the pub after work, so quite soon the athlete was nearer 18 stone and ready to take to the roads.

At first he kept on his ordinary clothes though... so that he could break into a walk if anyone came along. But one day he came round a corner at a fair bit speed and before he could stop was clearly spied by Billy Thomson and his wife. He might have known they'd be in their garden on a Sunday afternoon. However Sandy's quick wit enabled him to hang on to his secret a bit longer. "Ye hinna seen a puckle stots have ye? That new baillie's left the gate open, damn him." By Christmas time, though, the thing was becoming too serious and could no longer be hidden.

Mrs Strachan was fair fed up with Sandy for coming home with his working clothes all lathered in sweat so she bought him a track suit. It was bright orange and very tight fitting and even at seventeen and a half stones, Sandy was a spectacular sight.

Sandy had to put up with the ribald laughter of the country-side: "Are ye comin or goin, Sandy?" they would say as he peched along. And heads were shaken. "Ye'll dae yersel a mischief Sandy Strachan." But worst of all was the dogs' abuse he had to suffer and that wasn't just the being yapped at that all joggers have to endure: you see Sandy had heard that in a Marathon race you got a drink every three miles, so he determined to try a five-mile trot with a drink plunked waiting for him at three miles.

The sun was beating down on him that day and the sweat lashing out of his sixteen and a half stone. The athlete was sustained by the thought of that drink. But when at last he came in sight of his oasis there, walking her dachshund, was dear old Miss Barr. Would the dear little creature see his polystyrene cup of nectar... sure enough Tricky saw, sniffed, dismissed the object as inedible and lifted a short back leg. After that treatment Sandy didn't fancy his drink either and the last two miles were thirsty work.

Through all his trials (and there were many more than those of which I have told you) Sandy was sustained by his thrawnness and by the fear of the loss of all that money he had wagered. So he never seriously considered giving up. On the day of the Aberdeen Marathon in 1984 our hero was there at the start, weighing sixteen stone and looking a bit sheepish in a rather natty new pair of blue running shorts.

Sandy had a plan of action. He'd read in a running magazine that many runners burned themselves out by going too quickly at the start and he was determined not to make that mistake. He would start off really slowly and then after the first few miles he would ease off. That would do fine, for all he had to do to win his bets was to finish the race. It was a long and agonising story but I'll make it as brief as possible.

The first thing that happened was that the other two thousand competitors all ran off and left Sandy to paddle along mile after mile on his own. At first he poured with sweat but, despite the stops for water every three and a quarter miles, by the time he'd done ten miles, Sandy had stopped sweating; he was quite dried out.

By the time he had reached half way he was walking most of the time and only breaking into a trot when anybody was looking - and down the hills. Mind you, even those bursts weren't that fast; on one of his sprints Sandy was overtaken by an old lady pushing a pram. But he stuck it out and kept going until, with 20 miles behind him, the athlete was looking so grim that the ambulance men stopped and asked if he was alright. "Certainly," he growled furious, dizzy and sore. "I aye look like this." The ambulance followed him all the way in but Sandy refused a lift, even when cramp set in in both his legs.

Now, if you're an athlete there's nothing to a marathon really; it's all over in less than two and a half hours. But Sandy Strachan had been going for fully six and a quarter hours when he crossed the finishing line and fell in a dazed but triumphant heap. He'd done it, he'd shown them, and he'd won all those bets. "What was my time?" he croaked to the ambulance men as they wrapped him up and bundled him in. "Oh ye winna get a time. They packed up the clock at six hours." "Well I'll need to go for my medal," said Sandy trying to rise. "Oh you canna get a medal without a time," said the ambulance man.

CHAPTER SIX

# A Christian Burial

THE REVEREND Wilson Dunbar was walking by the river - he always did when things had been going wrong, or his life in the small country living provided by the Church of Scotland for the minister of Draven Parish became particularly difficult.

Certainly it was an ideal place for a walk on one of those few warm days you get near Scotland's North-east coast. The path that followed the north bank of the river Tealon was too rough to be plagued by cars and for some reason even those dreadful youths with their motor bikes seemed always to do their rallying elsewhere. There had been a wood there until it was cut down in 1942 as part of the war effort and it had never been replanted. Nor had it been ploughed. And there's no doubt the moor could have been ploughed with profit, for it had been before. When the trees had been cut down, that had revealed a series of regular undulations in the ground which an expert from the University said were among the finest example of corn-rigs in all Scotland. If our forefathers could cultivate the Tealon Moor with the ploughs available in the 17th century, the moor could easily have been returned to the plough in the second half of the 20th. It never had been, though, and for no better reason than that the farmer wanted to keep a few hill cows and was eligible for the hill cow subsidy.

So, with the rigs and the few scattered pine trees which remained as testimony to the fact that it had once been part of the great Caledonian Forest, the place had a feeling of history about it. If you took your troubles to a place like that, maybe they didn't seem so bad.

"But," you will surely think, "a man like Wilson Dunbar wouldn't often need to seek the solace offered by the Tealon Moor." After all, even in 1987 the minister, even in that small village in Aberdeenshire, had most of what it takes to make a man happy (or at least most of the things men strive for in the belief that they will make them happy). He was a respected figure in the community - one of the very few who was called "Mr", even by the laird. And, if his stipend was far from generous, it was, with the bit of money that Mrs Dunbar had brought to their marriage, quite enough for their needs. They had the manse to live in and, if that was cold and draughty all winter, it was alright most of the summer and, with its commanding position in the village, it was an impressive residence all the year round - and by any standard.

And you couldn't say the Reverend Dunbar was over-worked; not that, as some people thought, the minister only worked one day a week. Of course he had to visit the sick, comfort the bereaved and bring succour to the poor. But there had never been many poor in Draven and the Welfare State and the oil boom had all but eliminated poverty. Draven folk were hardly ever sick and, although the death rate was the same in Draven as anywhere else (everyone died once), there always seemed to be a big gap between funerals.

Not only that but the Draveners were a fairly godless lot. Oh they were Christians alright, and members of the Kirk, but their requirements of their God and their demands of his representative in the village were limited, in most cases to thrice in a lifetime: the typical parishioner of Draven wanted a church wedding, a church funeral and, though this might be less important, increasing numbers in the village had, in recent years, expressed a preference for having their children christened in the Kirk. In return for those three vital services, the average Christian in Draven was willing to turn up a further twice a year; on the two Sundays when Holy Communion was celebrated. On all other Sundays the Reverend Wison Dunbar preached to a congregation which he chose to call "select".

This state of affairs, though hardly a model of devotion, suited most of the village just fine. While the select few enjoyed their moral superiority, the majority got all they wanted from their church.

But the Reverend Dunbar was not happy about the Draveners' casual approach to their maker. When the young Dunbar had received his calling it had been to share with his parish the Communion of Saints and lead them in Christian worship and fellowship. Some of the ministers round about might make their own compromises, but the minister of Draven Parish Church would not see himself as a poorly paid social worker who could be called upon to put on an elaborate charade to adorn two happy occasions and one miserable one for every Tom, Dick and Harry in the parish. Goodness me! one of his elders in the parish had told him just the other day that two reputedly staunch members of his congregation had been discussing the price of barley right in the middle of a graveside service.

No, no. The Reverend Wison Dunbar wouldn't accept that sort of thing for he was a man of principle. It was those principles that had led him once again to the walk by the Tealon water, and it had all blown up over a man who wasn't even in the Kirk.

Johnny Miller was, in descending order of importance in bringing the scorn of the good people of Draven upon him, a socialist, a hunchback, a crofter and an atheist. He didn't even go to Communion for Johnny wasn't a hypocrite. Any time he had gone to church, and of course that was every Sunday as a child, he hadn't discussed the price of barley. He had listened attentively. The trouble was he hadn't thought much of what he had heard. And the atheistic crofter had often crossed swords with the minister from whom he had very different ideas about the power of prayer. Everybody knew about the time Mr Dunbar tackled Johnny on why he'd been spreading manure one Sunday in April instead of taking Communion like the rest of the parish.

"Well, minister, I'll tell you what we'll dae. We'll tak a park each. You pray a' that you can and I'll try a couple of tons of nitrogen. The winner'll be the een wi the best crop."

On the other hand, the minister had no such cheek to put up

with from the rest of the Miller family, for Johnny's brother and sister were part of Draven's moral minority. Indeed his big brother, Alexander, was an elder and no one who knew her could have doubted that the formidable Isabella Middleton, as she had now become, would have been an elder too, if they'd had that sort of thing in Draven. Mind you if she had been an elder she'd have had to take Communion with the godless hoard at the morning service on Communion days and she wouldn't have liked that. For, while Isabella never missed morning service on any other day, she preferred to avoid the chattering hoards, with their rustling sweetie papers, by taking Communion in the quieter evening service.

Old John Miller had been a member of the Free Church until it closed its doors before the war and he'd believed that a good dose of hell fire and damnation was essential to a good upbringing. But, while the faith thus instilled had stuck with Alexander and Isabella, Johnny had rebelled, and there were those who said that was all he could do - poor misshapen get that he was.

As you can well appreciate, Johnny's atheism had been a sore trial to his brother and sister while he lived. So, while it would hardly be fair to say that his death came as a relief to his siblings, they did have the consolation that his opposition to the church of their fathers could hardly extend beyond his death; they would at least be able to give him a Christian burial.

Or so they thought. For they had reckoned without the conscience of the Reverend Wilson Dunbar who, having been notably unsuccessful in getting people into his church, was now determined to keep this one out.

"I'm sorry, Mr Miller, but there is no account upon which I could give your brother a full funeral service in Church. It would be quite inappropriate for one who avoided worship in his life to be the centre of worship in his death. No, the best I can offer is a few words at the graveside - and not the usual form of words you understand. I couldn't possibly say, for example, that we were burying poor John 'in the sure and certain hope of his resurrection to eternal life'."

Few men can have done their duty with a feebler perception of the consequences for their own peace of mind. You could never have kept a secret like that for very long, of course, but with the brother and sister's sorrow, shame and rage, the scandal spread as only scandal in a Scottish village can spread. Johnny had been found on Saturday morning slumped on the seat of his old Fergie tractor. By late afternoon Isabella's wailing, which seemed quite out of proportion to the loss to such a formidable woman of so wayward a brother, had sounded the alert. And by early evening Alexander's need for something to steady his nerves had turned out to be so considerable that he had told everyone in Craigie's bar. And that, as everybody knew, was far better than getting it on the B.B.C.

Once Alexander got started it all came pouring out. "The injustice of it. Did his seventeen years as an elder count for nothing that he couldn't even get a decent burial for his own brother? And how come the minister of Garmont, not seven miles away, had even buried a Catholic never mind a simple non-attender? And what would folk say?"

Well, Alexander wasn't left long to wonder on the last score for the good people of Draven were more than willing to make their views known. "It was a damned shame to keep a harmless soul like Johnny from a decent burial when you think of some that's been let in. Johnny might have got real fu' most years at the Flower Show dance but look at the old doctor - he had been an alcoholic. And Annie Crighton that had had a bairn before she was married, got her mother to bring it up and from the day she did get married crossed the road rather than speak to her own son - the minister buried her alright." And more than one referred to that dirty old devil Mackenzie who couldn't keep his hands to himself - and him an elder and collecting for the church when he'd given that lassie a scare in her own house - and how it had taken near the whole Kirk Session to keep the parents from telling the police. "No doubt one day Dunbar'll be saying good riddance to Alec Mackenzie 'in the sure and certain hope for his resurrection to eternal life'." And poor Johnny wasn't to get in and him such a workhorse at all the church dos, like the sale of work and the bairns' Fun Day. "And wasn't it Johnny who had put the big farmers to shame by putting up one of his three heifers for the roup in aid of the Kirk roof?"

"Aye," as Craigie the publican himself put it, "there's nothing quite so unforgiving as a Christian."

But many in the village supported the minister's stand. Like the Miss Piries who had been horrified years ago when the young Mr Dunbar had put a doll in the church at Christmas time. That had been sheer idolatry. But now the minister had learned sense and was for no more Godlessness in his Kirk.

"How are you going to get decent folk to go to the Kirk," the younger Miss Pirie had opined, "if anybody can get a kirk funeral ?... or a wedding for that matter? If Humpy Johnny wanted a Kirk funeral he could have gone to the Kirk like any decent body."

When the Reverend Wilson Dunbar heard that fervour of religious debate in his parish had reached such a pitch that Craigie's bar had had to close early and that one of his senior elders had only narrowly escaped arrest, he resolved to start Sunday's sermon by putting the record straight. And thus he spoke before a congregation that was much bigger, much more attentive and, on the whole, much more hostile than that to which he was used.

"It would be quite inappropriate" he said, "for us to have a funeral service for the late John Miller. That service is the Christian's way of thanking God for the Christian fellowship he's enjoyed with the deceased. It's held to the glorification of God and the comfort of those left behind. The presence of the body of an atheist at such a ceremony would be meaningless in terms of the gospels. In any case the body is only a body - for the spirit of John Miller has already gone - where it has gone. It is no part of my job to give him what I know some people call 'a good send-off'. Let us pray."

But that was by no means that.

The debate raged on. It was a difficult time for the minister, though, in the gentlemanly way of these people, most of the unkind things that were said about him were said behind his back. Alexander announced his resignation as an elder and several other elders threatened to do the same. But there was no easy way out, for at least two others said they would resign if Mr Dunbar changed his mind. More than a dozen families determined to shift their lines to neighbouring parishes if Johnny's remains weren't allowed into the Kirk and no doubt there were others who would have moved had the minister given in.

Several of the most important figures in Draven undertook to 'have a word with Dunbar' - people with influence and money - the sort who are used to getting their own way.

"Now look here, Mr Dunbar, you said yourself that the funeral service was for the comfort of those left behind. Well surely we should offer the Millers what comfort we can. After all, they're staunch church-goers themselves. And it's not the atheist who's wanting in, Minister, it's his Christian relatives that want a church service. No Minister, I don't agree (and what a thing for you to say anyway) - that we should respect the views of an atheist and not let his relatives give him a Christian burial. After all, if he's right that there's nothing after death he canna very well mind what we do with his remains - and if we Christians are right about the hereafter then surely the Christian thing is to do our best for him. And surely you could relent and let some other minister into our church to take the service. And, as you know Minister, you've buried a lot worse than Johnny Miller."

But it was all to no avail and on a cold Tuesday in February the biggest crowd ever seen in the Draven kirkyard saw Johnny Miller's coffin lowered into the ground. And, as his brother and sister tried to hold back tears of shame and disillusion, the Reverend Dunbar expressed the hope that a merciful God would live up to his reputation in respect of John Miller.

The Reverend Wilson Dunbar was surprised to be invited by the old established legal firm of Ogston and Shand to the reading of the will of John Smith Miller. His greetings to Alexander and Isabella were, frankly, embarrassed.

"It's an interesting will," said old Mr Ogston excitedly. "I've never seen one quite like it. I've been looking forward to the day when I could share its contents with you. Oh! My goodness. I'm sorry Mrs Middleton and Mr Miller, I eh... well.... this is what it says after the usual preliminaries:

"As is well known, I've never believed in God but I've always believed strongly in the Kirk. It helps the young to see the importance of what they're getting themselves into, to stand up before all their friends and relations and have the words that have stood the ravages of time and reason, said over them, and people need something to do in times of grief and the rigmarole and the singing those sincere old songs about a mystery of life are just what those who are left behind need. And a good going kirk is vital to the life of a village. Look what's happened to Old Mayne. Now that it's lost its kirk it's not a village any more... just a collection of houses. If you took away the kirk dos and the carol singing round the doors, how much less would Draven be a centre for folk's lives. Even kirk attendance itself... it gives you a chance to get out and meet folk... an excuse in the hurly burly of life to slow down, put on your best and go down to the village. Of course I never went much, though I fine like to sing, but then, even in my best clothes, I never looked that good.

"In consideration of all that, and the sure and certain knowledge of the great comfort the Kirk will have been to my dear brother and sister as they disposed of the brother they surely loved but never understood, and, as they have both provided well for themselves, I hereby leave the proceeds of the croft and the stock and machinery and household effects, after Isabella and Alexander have taken any keepsake they may wish, to the Church of Scotland."

So the Reverend Wilson Dunbar needed his walk by the river Tealon to work things out. Had he been right to stick to his principles or was he, like those few trees on Tealon Moor, no more than a reminder of times past?

CHAPTER SEVEN

# The Grieve from Rhynie

WHEN THE definitive history of Scottish Agriculture is written
there will surely be a central chapter for the grieves. Those hard
men who, by example and by their own particular brand of terror,
managed to persuade more work, better done than could ever be
reasonable, out of those who laboured on the land. One of my
favourite stories about them is about the grieve at Drumdelgie -
then, as now, one of the biggest farms in the North-east. Someone
asked Drumdelgie's grieve how it was that, with those enormous
parks, he always managed to have the men at the near end of the
parks at lousin time.

"Aha, laddie," said the grieve, "if ye only kent the answer tae
that ye'd be man enough to be grieve at Drumdelgie."

They were a bit like that, the old-fashioned grieves. There
was only one way to do a job and that was to do it the right way;
and you never got the better of a grieve. Jock Paterson was one of
the great grieves of Aberdeenshire, of whom it was once said:
"They are a group of potential Prime Ministers but with far more
important things to do."

Well, Jock's reign of terror lasted from the 1930s to the
1950s, at Milton of Noth near Huntly, and was typified by his
remark about a ploughman who was by common consent a most
excellent worker.

"Nae use ava - he's the lad that gings awa in the middle o'
hairst."

And the man's crime? He'd been in agony with toothache and had taken the afternoon in harvest time to bike the 16 miles into Huntly to have three teeth extracted - without anaesthetic - and had been back in time to do a bit of stooking after his supper.

But to our tale. It was in the winter of 1947, about the fifth week of the great storm, and tempers were getting short. They were feeding a lot of cattle that year at Milton of Noth and to help with that, one of the great labour-saving devices on such a modern farm was a motorised neep-hasher for cutting up the turnips so they were easier for the cattle to eat.

It was a Barclay, Ross and Hutchison, petrol driven, air-cooled job with great blades which slashed through the neeps as you graiped them in over. And as the neeps wore down the shed the cattlemen could, with difficulty, by tugging at the shafts beside the engine, shoogle it down the neep shed.

With the best will in the world - on the part of the baillie - this priceless asset would break down from time to time as the blades broke on stray stones that were graiped in with the turnips. Well, that happened on the fifth week of the great storm of 1947 and Jock Paterson the grieve was not amused. 'It was nae use ava... pure carelessness... t'hell did he think he was deein?'... and so on and so on. The grieve sent the third horseman and the loon, with a horse yoked between those awkward shafts, down through the snow to the smiddy at Rhynie.

Now it was the grieve's job to have the hasher back ready for action when it was next needed, and here the baillie, Louis Gray, thought he saw his chance to get one back at Jock. At five o' clock he met the grieve in the close:

"I'll be needin that hasher at 7 o' clock the morn's morning."

He knew the grieve would lose face if the machine wasn't home for the morning, or if he had to yoke a horse after it had been lowsed.

The baillie went whistling off to his supper. But when he met the grieve in the close the next morning he was astonished when told, "Your hasher's in the neep shed".

He had not reckoned on the determination and pride of Jock Paterson, which had led him to perform a legendary feat of endurance, and given him the strength for it.

After his supper the grieve had gone down to the Richmond Arms at Rhynie, had a tremendous night among the drams with his friend Sandy McIntosh the miller, and then set about manhandling the neep hasher home. The hasher was about as awkward a thing as you could imagine, with its shafts wide enough for a horse. It weighed four-and-a-half hundredweight and the baillies needed a great effort to move it a couple of yards down the neepshed. And yet, with the strength that pride and drams and being a grieve could give, Jock Paterson hauled and shoved the neep hasher over a mile home to Milton of Noth through the storm, and rose the next morning as though nothing had happened.

# CHAPTER EIGHT

# *The Vatman*

THIS STORY is about a heroic and successful defence of one of
Scottish farming's finest traditions.

The tradition in question is the liberal interpretation of the
licensing laws which for many years enabled farmers to consume
alcoholic beverages in the General Merchants (as the local super-
markets used to be called). If you felt like a clandestine drink you
just went into the right shop, announced that you wanted to buy
nails and, with no more than a sly nod, you'd be shown through
to the back shop and served with your pleasure. The facility of
buying nails was, of course, much more important in the days
before the war when rural Scotland had fewer pubs and bigger
thirsts. In those days, some of the country's most notable farmers
spent a considerable portion of their week scouring the countryside for nails. It's much reduced now of course, but despite that
nasty shock in the early 1970s it still persists in at least one
Scottish village. And it's really no wonder for it was an attractive
tradition.

You got a fine atmosphere in the back shop as the strong
smell of Bogey Roll mingled with language that was even
stronger. Ladies never bought nails so it was an all-male society,
a sort of poor man's Oxford Union, where the important issues of
the day were thrashed out with one's peers in circumstances that
were, if not that comfortable, at least more congenial than being
back on the farm doing what the wife thought you were doing.

No-one knew you were drinking, though they might suspect, for what could be more innocent than your car parked outside the General Merchant's, so it was better than the pub even where there was one. It also had the advantage of providing a way round the licensing laws in the days before all-day drinking in Scotland, and better than that, it was a way of getting a much-needed refresher through the books. Nails, you see, were always sold on credit and were charged along with the half-yearly bills for fencing wire, baling twine and the like... and why shouldn't the farm pay for the drink? After all, it was the farm that made a man thirsty in the first place.

But what nearly ruined this fine tradition was the introduction in 1973 of the dreaded Value Added Tax. Now it wasn't that the farmers of Scotland's North-east were greedily trying to get the Vatman to subsidise their drinking, though goodness knows some of them could have used all the help they could get. It was more that the wives do the Vat returns on so many farms. The men had no doubt neglected to tell their loved ones that invoices for nails should be treated with discretion, especially if they ran well into three figures for the half year.

But it wasn't so much the huge quantities of nails that were appearing in the farmers' books that gave the game away. It was when the Vatman found that the General Merchant in Graivel was selling fifty times as many nails as he was buying.

Nothing would make Simon MacAskill (the young, keen and unfortunately highly principled) Vatman see sense and leave well alone. Simon Pure, as he soon came to be called, with an uncharacteristic lack of originality but a wholly predictable lack of affection, was determined to go all the way with this one. It was his first big case. Huge penalties were confidently expected and the shopkeeper would surely go to jail.

Consternation reigned in the village. It wasn't just the fines and the possibility of jail that were upsetting, nor the reputations that were at stake (several of the nail buyers were elders of the Kirk). It was far more serious than that; a whole way of life was threatened.

Now you may well have heard of the Scottish farming Mafia. It's nothing like its Sicilian counterpart really. It's mainly a political and social thing; the Scottish farming mobsters don't go around shooting people... but generations of horse dealing have made them masters of the offer that can't be refused. And it was decided that Simon Pure be made such an offer.

I don't know the exact details of how it was done (these things are always handled with such discretion) but it went something like this:

The young Vatman was inveigled by the offer of lunch into the pub in the neighbouring village. A virtual non-drinker, he was persuaded to accept a half pint of cider which, by mistake, turned out to be a pint. He'd allowed himself a glass of wine with the meal and, fatally perhaps, two helpings of Miss Macpherson's fearsome sherry trifle.

As Simon MacAskill fastened himself into his metallic blue Mini-Metro he felt distinctly mellow... but not for long. He couldn't even remember if he'd got started when round the corner, going much too fast in reverse, came a white Cortina. The damage wasn't extensive and Simon was all for a quick exchange of insurance companies and off. But the other driver would have none of that. It was his wife's car and he would need to get it repaired properly; and he'd such a bad record that his insurance company insisted on a police report of all his accidents. And anyway, as it was the back of his car that was damaged, the police would certainly say that it was Simon's fault. And of course there would be the breathalyser. And while the farmer would have liked to let the matter drop, he really couldn't afford to as he was one of those that were facing huge penalties for defrauding the Vatman.

Now, Simon MacAskill may have lived a life sheltered from a cruel world by the love of his considerable mother and by the moral certainty that she had instilled into him, but he wasn't so green that he couldn't recognise blackmail when he got close to it... nor was he so dim as to fail to see that they'd got him. It was clear, even to the lad who in his short life had yet to experience sin at first hand, that either his job (which required him to drive) or his principles would have to go.

Things looked black for Simon MacAskill.

But, like honest men of principle the world over and since time began, when faced with economic disaster, a thorough examination of his conscience revealed that the paths of righteousness were nothing like as straight nor so narrow as he had formerly believed.

"Well... there's no doubt this buying of nails will have to stop. We can't have you farmers claiming back the value-added tax on your..eh... refreshment bills. But I suppose if you were to change from nails to something that was zero-rated, there would be no harm in it... from a V.A.T. point of view."

So nowadays if you're doing a morning's shopping in the General Merchant's at Graivel, especially in that thirsty hour between ten-thirty and eleven-thirty, don't be surprised to find a farmer come in, say that he's come to pay for his newspapers and then disappear into the back shop.

If you have a discerning ear you may be able to hear the murmur of earnest conversation and even the clink of the odd glass.

CHAPTER NINE

# *LOUISA*

NATURE IS a weird and wonderful thing, and it's never weirder nor more wonderful than when we farmers start mucking about with it. This is a true story and it happened at Little Ardo in 1974. It is an example of mothering instinct and filial love which defies all my attempts at scientific explanation.

We had imported this Gelbvieh cow from Germany. But unfortunately Louisa, as she was called, didn't like the bull, or perhaps it was that she liked him too well for every three weeks she came back in season. Now Louisa was worth about five ordinary cows (at least that's what it cost me to import her from Germany), and I was very keen indeed that she be in calf.

So we decided to put Louisa in for transplanting. That's the technique for getting more than one calf per year out of cows by using surrogate mothers. It's just the same as surrogate motherhood in humans, just about as expensive but not so surrounded by scandal. So off went Louisa down to England for transplanting.

The first step was an injection to make her produce more than one egg - the same sort of fertility drug that made those ladies produce all those multiple births we heard of a few years back.

They then inseminated Louisa and took four fertilised eggs out of her and put them into four cross heifers who then bore them to term. Two months later they tried the same thing again, but it didn't work so we got her home again, where we succeeded in putting her in calf.

My deal with the transplanting company was that they would do the job for nothing in return for half the calves. So in due course we got the two cross heifers home - each five months pregnant with one of Louisa's calves while Louisa was also in calf, though she was about four months behind the others.

In the fullness of time the two foster mothers produced a fine bull calf each and Louisa was a mother of two babies, but still only five months in calf.

Now the extraordinary thing is that Louisa, who couldn't know about transplants, proceeded to claim her calves.

When her fostered calves were born, she made a bag of milk that would have done a Friesian proud, although she was only five months in calf herself.

Well, Louisa suckled those two calves for four months until

she calved our third little Gelbvieh bull, and then we separated them. The older calves had had the sense to keep their foster mothers going as well, so the whole thing worked out just fine.

But why did it happen? You often get a cow bagging up early. And it is not uncommon for calves to suck the wrong cow. But there were ten calving heifers in that field and Louisa was the only one that produced early milk. And there were about twelve calves in that field and only two of them sucked the wrong cow.

No, no. Louisa knew her calves and probably they knew her.

I often used to see Louisa standing in the corner of the field with a faraway look in her eyes. I wondered if she was worrying about her third and fourth fostered babies, who were born in England. If only I had been able to speak the German I could have told her. One was a heifer and one was a bull and they both went to America. But I think she already knew. I'm sure Louisa knew.

# CHAPTER TEN

# *The Auctioneer*

YOU DON'T often find auctioneers who are snappy dressers; they're usually very conventional, dowdy even, as though they didn't want their profits to show. But not so Alexander McIlraith. He was a renowned dandy all his days and acquired an accent to match. He'd not had a public school education (and of course there wasn't an R.A.F. when he was a young man) but by catholic reading and careful observation, he'd assumed the dress, manner and bearing of an Old Etonian or at the very least an Old Fettesian. 'Mr Alexander', as he was known by the clerks and secretaries wore a bowler hat, good tweed suits, spats and (without fail) a red rose in his buttonhole.

He worked for the old auctioneering firm of McIlraith and Addison. They've been taken over, like so many of the other small firms, by one of the big combines now but for many years they served the area around Creath as only a family firm in a tight-knit community can. 'M and A' bought and sold every-thing: farms, land, furniture, grain, shootings and you name it. They did valuations, arbitrations and displenishes and always for a commission which didn't seem cheap but wasn't quite high enough to make it worth while getting another firm in.

But McIlraith and Addison's main business was, of course, livestock. They would arrange for batches of dairy calves to be delivered from the big farms around Aberdeen and even Dundee. They brought sheep down from the Shetlands and Caithness to be fattened, and they even brought some of those great big black and white stots over from Canada for finishing. But where 'M and A' served their area best was in selling young stock from the thin hard lands of Glen Fedderate and the Larnach as stores to be fattened on the rich flat farms around Creath.

Alexander McIlraith had worked hard in the firm as a young man but by the 1930s he was in his sixties, the senior partner, and had the job well enough organised to allow him to practise the style he had so carefully cultivated, the style of a gentleman. All the serious hard work (like the auctioneering itself) was left to men who were both younger and poorer, but true to the tradition of the family firm, Mr Alexander insisted on visiting each of his clients every year - 'the personal touch don't you know'.

The farmers and crofters of Glen Fedderate got their 'personal touch' each spring when the dandy auctioneer came canvassing for the store sales; to see how many lambs there would be for the summer sales, how many calves there would be for the calf sales and how many ewes they might be casting.

Well now, on this occasion Mr Alexander had been canvassing at a little croft at the head of the Glen. He'd done some business; there'd be twenty-seven lambs, mostly for the second sale, and two suckled calves for September. Then came the personal contact in which McIlraith and Addison so prided themselves and which went so much further than mere commerce, "And how's your good lady... er... Mr McDonald?" said the carefully cultivated voice.

"Oh well did ye nae see it in the papers? I doubt she's deed."

"Oh dear me, I am sorry to hear that. You poor fellow. How are you managing?"

"Oh well, Annie, she's thirteen, she's left the school to gie me a hand wi the three bairns and we're just managin awa as best we can," said the crofter.

"Jolly good, well done, stout fellow..." and off went the dandy auctioneer on his royal tour.

A year passed and Mr Alexander was back at McDonald's croft and another consignment of calves and lambs had been agreed. The auctioneer was almost ready to go:

"And how's your good lady, Mr... er... McDonald?" he said.

"Aye, mind I tell't ye last year... she's deed... and how Annie had to leave the school to help look efter the bairns," said the crofter patiently.

"Yes, yes. Yes indeed and you're managing fine. Grand, grand. Well I hope to see you at the sales." He always said that but he never did see McDonald at the sales, though the crofter always saw him.

When the dandy auctioneer's Lagonda brought him back the next year the same lugubrious performance was enacted. Twenty-two lambs would be sold as stores, there would be three calves for the suckled calf sale in September, and the old cow would go to the farrow ring when her calf was spent at the end of August.

"And how's your good lady?" said Alexander McIlraith, with the usual show of intense interest.

"Oh, she's still deed," said Willie McDonald.

## CHAPTER ELEVEN

# *The White Settler*

NIGEL McCROAN had a dream.... A few acres in the country, a very well paid job in town and a wife who would be both young and beautiful to dance attention on his every whim.

Sheer brass neck and catching her young and foolish enough, when he was old and sly enough, got him a truly beautiful wife who at least was young to start with and would always be younger than him. And the North Sea oil boom gave him the chance to rise from virtually nothing to a £60,000 a year driller on an oil rig. So by 1980 he was ready to realise the third part of his dream and he soon purchased the 60 acre farm of Backhill of Myriedubbs.

"Good name that," he thought, "Nothing Johnny-Come-Lately about a name like that... very Scottish." He never thought the place might have got its name because it was a muddy swamp and off the beaten track... but he was to find out.

The first step in stage two was to get the Range-Rover, for Nigel had always seen the white Rangie as part and parcel of the lifestyle of the country gentleman. He didn't notice that the Range-Rover set weren't farming places like Backhill of Myriedubbs. However the Rangie did arrive about the same time as the Barbour jacket, the Purdeys and the green wellies.

Next came the cow, for Nigel wasn't just going to become a country gentleman, he would return to the natural goodness of things. There would be no more milk from a plastic cow, all cold and collected from the supermarket.

He would keep a few pigs too. They would eat up the scraps and they would look fine rooting about in the field in front of the house.

And eggs - they would keep their own hens of course, but they certainly wouldn't keep them in that old hen battery. That was a really cruel way to keep animals.

"How stupid other farmers are," Nigel thought "not to realise how much better eggs you get on a free-range system. And that way it costs you less because the hens feed themselves naturally on seeds at the roadside or worms in the grass." Poultry was clearly a good idea so when they were offered a bantie hen with five goslings Nigel just couldn't resist.

"Oh yes, Christmas will be really good this year at Backhill of Myriedubbs."

A horse? Of course, a man like Nigel McCroan would need a horse even if he couldn't ride. He bought a big one all the same and was pleased when the dealer said it was a spirited gelding.

And then there was the garden. Old Jeannie Taylor had kept it beautifully. She'd had a good bit lawn at the front with a diamond shaped rose bed in the middle and a border of peri-winkles and pansies right round it. There were fruit bushes at the back beside the strawberry beds and, at the side of the house, the kitchen garden. The beautiful Elizabeth would keep them going with real fresh country fruit and vegetables. And, what's more, she'd do it without all those chemicals other people used to force extra growth and kill all those creepy crawlies. Nigel and Elizabeth had no doubt whatsoever but that their lives were all set to enter an idyllic phase at Backhill of Myriedubbs.

But, if you're a farmer or even someone who knows a bit about the countryside, you'll have seen some at least of the flaws in his plan.

The trouble started when Myrtle the cow arrived. Nigel had gone to the Kittybrewster mart and bought the sappiest looking Friesian he could find. One of the drovers had shown him how to get the milk out but Nigel's milking was slow and rough - Myrtle was used to a machine anyway and she kicked the aspiring milk-maid clean across the byre, though 'clean' wasn't the word that came to mind when Nigel picked himself up. The sight of him made Elizabeth laugh and that made Nigel say something he was to say often in the difficult days that lay ahead:

"Shut up, you fool," he rasped.

Despite the cow's unco-operation Nigel eventually did get the best part of a pint of milk and it was with some pride of achievement that he bore it into the house.

"That'll be quite enough for the coffee," he said.

And so it might have been but it certainly wasn't enough for Myrtle. She was used to giving thirty-two pints of milk and twice a day at that. The poor cow was left stiff, sore and leaking, and she let them know about that by roaring at them all night.

It's well known that milking's a woman's job anyway, so after that Elizabeth got the milking to do.

"And see if you can do something right for a change," he soured at her.

The pigs were a bit of a problem too. Nigel had insisted that it was cruel to put rings in pigs' noses without bothering to find out what those were for. But he soon found out for, uninhibited by fears of a sore snout, the pigs ploughed the little field in front of the house. Then they got into the garden and ploughed Elizabeth's lawn.

"Oh, the horrible brutes," wailed the beautiful Elizabeth. "Please, Nigel, please put rings in their noses."

"Shut up you fool," came the reply, "and why couldn't you shut the gate, anyway?"

Nigel's free-range hens weren't a great success either. They seemed to range mostly in the barley he'd had sown for him by a contractor and the budding farmer seemed to spend half his time shooing them out. He didn't realise that a dozen hens weren't going to make much of an impact on a forty acre field anyway. But it wasn't so much the barley they ate as they free-ranged at Backhill that upset Elizabeth. She just hated the little deposits they left everywhere, especially on the doorstep, and she was told to shut up and that she was a fool when she complained that the hens were scratching up her lettuce seeds. Mind you, if the hens had scratched up more of Elizabeth's seeds they might have spared their mistress another bawling out. That wet summer was a bad one for growing your own lettuce even for people who did use slug pellets and of course the McCroans would never have used anything so unnatural. So what with all this farming to do, as well as the house, she made a poor job of washing the lettuce and Nigel got his teeth into a bit that was just too organic. He wasn't pleased, or even tolerant.

"Can't you do anything?" he bawled. "I'm going off-shore tomorrow and when I get back I want to see this place properly organized. Clean the cow shed and stop feeding Myrtle so much and then she'll maybe make less milk. Fix that gate and mend the fence in front of the house. Keep your hens off my barley and don't you dare use my Range-Rover." And when poor Elizabeth tried to speak: "Shut up, you fool."

Life at Backhill was not living up to expectations.

Even the horse - or maybe I should say especially the horse - hadn't been a success. Nigel made a rare sight on the first day; jodhpurs which, despite being enormous, were full to overflowing, Prior-Palmer hat and a very expensive-looking bone-handled riding crop. I think it was with the riding crop that Nigel made his big mistake. Sultan had seen this type before. He didn't throw him but made sure Nigel never got up again. It is a fact, you see, that in a five-acre field it is impossible for an unpleasant oilman to catch a wise and unwilling horse.

I can't say I was sorry, though I did like Elizabeth, but I lost touch with the McCroans for a couple of years. When I did have occasion to drop by, Nigel told me the rest of the story. The hens had given a few delicious eggs at, he'd calculated, about a pound a piece and he'd never tried keeping pigs again. He'd discovered what any of his neighbours could have told a good listener: that you can't fatten modern pigs on scraps. The geese had thriven though until, wakened by their dawn chorus and driven mad with a hangover, he'd shot them. The contractor had always been too busy to come at the right times and the crops had been a disaster. Myrtle the cow was gone... and so was the beautiful Elizabeth.

CHAPTER TWELVE

# Annie Garden's Wedding

WELL, THIS is it. After all the preparations, Annie Garden was in procession to the Parish Church. She was flanked by her sens, the two young men her intended had, by tradition, sent to her home to escort her. And she knew Martin Buchan would be approaching the church from the other side, if the two young maidens she'd sent for him had managed to get the groom's party roaded. If only the bride's party had been quiet for a minute they'd have had no difficulty hearing that the Buchans were on their way - but there was no chance of that, for the pipers were in good fettle by this time and all the Gardens who could raise a musket or a pistol were firing them off into the air. Fortunately though, the drams they'd had with their breakfast of porridge, curds and cream, were already slowing down the reloading time, despite the fact that it was not yet noon.

As she walked along between her strong young men, Annie had none of the apprehension a young bride might have had on the approach of a new life with a stranger. It was a beautiful sunny day - and that was just the latest in a long line of omens that meant this would be a good marriage.

Hadn't they taken a red-hot coal from the fire and placed two peas on it? And hadn't the peas both stayed on the coal and burned together rather than one of them rolling off to escape? And when she'd gone to the kailyard at Hallowe'en and pulled up that stalk of cabbage had the root not brought up a nice big clump of soil with it, promising prosperity in marriage to a good-looking young man? And Martin Buchan was certainly that, and of course Annie had seen Martin when she'd asked (three years earlier, when she was only sixteen) to have her future husband revealed to her.

She'd gone through the routine. She'd read the third verse of the seventeenth chapter of the Book of Job after supper, washed the supper dishes and gone to bed without a single word, stuck a pin in the verse she'd read and put the bible under her pillow.

According to her mother, her partner would be revealed and sure enough, the face she saw was Martin's. Mind you, there was very little else in Annie's head but Martin and she'd tried awful hard to see him whatever.

And now she was on the way with all her family to meet Martin for her kirkin. She'd been a wee bit worried about her dress fitting, because of course it was bad luck to try it on before the great day, but it fitted like a glove and she felt so bonnie when she left the house with her noisy party. And their first fit couldn't have been better for the first person they met on the road was Heilan' Willie mounted on his white garron - oh yes, they were right glad to give Willie his dram - a fact which Willie had known fine of course. Annie knew he knew but that made no difference on such a day.

They were met at the church door by the bellman and Annie was led to the bridesteel (as the bridal pew was called) where she met Martin for the first time that day. It was important that they didn't see each other before the church.

The ceremony; then for the young couple a time which seemed an age - and almost was, for there were many formalities to be accomplished - before they would be alone.

The minister kissed the bride and she pinned a favour on the Reverend's arm. The bellman got his saxpence and a collection was taken up from the congregation. Then, after endless congratulations, the two processions which had arrived at the church, formed up again and left as one for the groom's home, where the most enormous feast awaited them.

Most of the guests had contributed: a chicken here, a pig of whisky there, or a baking maybe. Mrs Buchan had made an enormous brew of ale and again the signs had been good - the froth had bubbled out at the near side rather than dribbling down the back (now that could have had something to do with the stick Martin had put under the cauldron to tilt it forward but, as his father had said, there's more to having good fortune than just being lucky).

Annie was welcomed at the door by her mother-in-law and had to enter under a sieve containing oatcakes and cheese - and while those were being eaten by the guests, the bride was led to the hearth where she kindled the fire. Then the crook from which the cooking pots hung over the fire was swung round 3 times in the name of the Father, the Son, and Holy Ghost, with the prayer 'Make this woman a good wife', and Annie's hand was plunged deep into the meal in the girnal as a sign for plenty in that house in times to come.

After considerable feasting and copious drinking, particularly of toddy drunk in numerous toasts, the dancing started with the Shannet Reel - a sixsome performed by the bride and groom and their best maidens and young men. And then the floor was open to jigging and reeling which sounded on into the small and not so small hours of the morning.

The young couple, hoping they'd been forgotten in all the revelry, tried twice to sneak off to their bed. It had been made up by Martin's married sister because she'd a young baby at the breast and that was considered lucky. And a fine bed it would be too, for Annie had been collecting her providan for three long years, and there was nothing but the finest gull's down in the bedding.

The first time, they were caught and brought back to the dance. The second time, the revellers took pity, but insisted on the ceremony of the beddin. The bride made ready and, once in bed, dispensed more cakes and ale to the revellers as though they were needing it. And then the young man made ready. Much play was made by the callants of the fact that Martin's feet were clean because of his friends washing them the night before. But Annie knew her loon washed his feet every week, wedding or no - even if they weren't needing it. His clean turn-out was one of the things that had attracted her.

When they were both abed the bride threw one of the stockings at the revellers and the most almighty drunken scramble ensued for the honour of getting the beddum hose.

After what seemed like an age, the last of them left and Martin and Annie were alone at last.

"And mind," said Martin, "the first one asleep dies first."

"Well I'm nae tired," said Annie, with a sweet little glint in her eye.

And there we'll draw a veil of discretion over the happy couple. But the marriage lived up to its promise, justified all the omens, and in another twenty years the Gardens and the Buchans were on their way to another kirkin, but this time they started from the same house.

# CHAPTER THIRTEEN

# A Fine Retirement Jobbie

OLD JIMMY had been grieve at Little Lendrum for thirty years when Littlie decided to call it a day. Jimmy couldn't imagine why his boss thought he needed to retire - God knew he'd never done a hand's turn about the place and had always left everything to his grieve; everything except the profit that is.

And there had always been plenty of that for James Low was a good farmer and a hard worker and expected his men to work as hard as he did. He always had the binder greased and ready the day before the crop was ripe; the courts were always waiting for the cattle on the first of November; and nothing that was needed was ever lost, or broken, or borrowed.

Maybe Jimmy had done too well in making Alec Duguid rich enough to retire, but that's what he did, on the 28th of November 1968. Now at 63 years of age, the grieve was just some old to be getting another job, and yet just young enough for the pension and a council house. And Duguid, old miser that he was, knew that just fine.

"Aye, Jimmy, you'll bide on for the roup and then be caretaker, kinda thing. I'll no be hard on you, but of course ye'll only get an orraman's wage... just a fine retirement jobbie for you."

Jimmy took Hobson's choice with an ill grace; it seemed an inauspicious way to run down fifty proud years of dedicated service... but what could he do?

Now the old grieve had, in common with most in that vocation, a thriving scepticism about the achievements of other farmers, but he had harboured an especially ill will at the farm of Netherton. The rivalry found expression at the bull sales and the cattle shows, for both places were in the Shorthorns in the great days of that breed. Many people thought Jimmy's attitude to everything about Netherton was some sort of sour grapes at some injustice he imagined he had suffered in the show ring, but in fact the antagonism had originated when Jimmy had given Netherton's grieve a hiding at the feeing market at Ellon in 1928. He never forgot, and certainly never forgave nor missed an opportunity to miscry 'Rough Netherton' as he called it.

Duguid's plan was to cash all his stock, put the land he'd been cropping down to grass, roup most of his machinery and rent out the grazing. Jimmy would see to the gates and the waterings and count the visiting cattle every day. That looked a sound enough plan to the grieve (now on an orraman's wage), but you can imagine his fury when he heard that, of all places, Rough Netherton had taken Little Lendrum's grass.

If there was any consolation, it lay in the heavy sarcasm to which Jimmy was able to give vent about Netherton's stock every spring when Netherton's dairy heifers arrived.

I witnessed one occasion: down came the tail door of the float. Jimmy took one look and said as loudly as he needed to:

"Oh aye, here they come, the walking wounded."

And he had a point, for attention to detail had never been Netherton's strong suit. The heifers were looking middling fair at best and Jimmy was just the man to tell them. He telephoned immediately.

"Hallo, Netherton here. Good morning."

"Aye, Little Lendrum. Ye'll need tae come doon and dose that heifers for worms."

"Oh dear, James, not looking as well as usual are they?"

"Aye jist about the usual... maybe waur."

"Oh very droll, James I'm sure. Let me see now. This is Thursday, busy day Friday. I'll tell you what, I'll send some of my

60

chaps down on Monday. How's that?"

"It's a' the same tae me," said Jimmy, "but if ye leave it or Monday it winna be such a big job."

Then there was the time he phoned about the heifers being in calf. They came down to Little Lendrum to grow, not to calve, and yet every year there were at least three in calf. The trouble was the great big Charolais bull Netherton had imported from France... Jimmy thought they must surely have no fences in France.

Well, this particular spring the heifers arrived as usual, and as usual Jimmy's quick eye spotted the calvers, four of them. He hastened to the phone.

"Netherton here, good morning."

"Little Lendrum. Ye'll need tae tak four o' yer heifers hame for they're in calf."

"No, no James," said the smooth and patronising voice, "that's quite impossible. The bull hasn't been near them you see."

"Oh aye," said Jimmy, "that's bloody funny than, for they look in calf tae me and there's twa feet stickin oot o' the back o' een o' them."

Jimmy fine liked to point out how incompetent Netherton's men were, but he didn't like the way they always made out somehow it was really his fault, and that he was bothering them. So, after that he stopped phoning.

What did it matter if a big place like that did lose the odd heifer? And Charolais cross calves sold well off the place... even for a quick deal.

# CHAPTER FOURTEEN

# *Fergus the Deer*

I DON'T SUPPOSE the red deer should have been taken off the hills in the first place. It would have been bad enough to have one monarch of the Glen suffer the indignity of life in the concrete prison which had been built for the Friesian bull in the days when Little Ardo was a dairy farm, but to have ten of them sharing its three metres by four was ridiculous. But there they were, the pioneers in the attempt in the early eighties, to do with deer what had for years been done with cattle and sheep. The hills would provide deer calves, just as they provided lambs and bovine calves, for fattening in the Lowlands.

It wasn't all bad in the bull's box. The ten stag calves dined royally on the best of hay and potatoes by the cart load, for there had been a surplus that year and the farmer could get all he wanted for stock feed at £5 a tonne. They got as much barley as they wanted, but what they really liked was household scraps - apple cores, outside leaves of lettuces and cabbages - and the weeds and surplus produce from the gardens of the little village of Methlick. A procession of folk from the village would arrive with little tributes - a handful of dandelions, some shot kale or best of all, some windfall apples.

So the calves grew well from the time they arrived in November until one fateful night the next September. It was not long after midnight when the door of the byre slid open. A dishevelled figure lurched into the shed, bonnet off the plumb, fag drooping, the beard well into its third day. The smell of drink filled the air and the smoke curled up and nipped the eyes.

He coughed. "I'll larn him to tak the lift o me," he said. Swinging open the door of the bull's box, he lurched off leaving the byre door open wide.

When you've been ten months in the cosy security of a bull's box you don't just bound out at the first open door, but by morning the young stags were taking their first look, for as long as they could remember, at the wider world.

They were scared by all the space they saw, but it was coming on to the rutting season and, while they didn't know what was missing, they knew that life in the bull's box was incomplete. Out they went - away from the safe walls which bounded their world into a great light, wide and scaring world. At first the ten huddled together and trotted nervously back and fore in a herd. But gradually they settled to graze the roadside. They enjoyed that. They'd had plenty of cut grass in the bull's box but this was the first growing grass they'd enjoyed since they were at their mothers' feet in the hills above Inverness - and growing grass is so much sweeter.

All developed well for the stags until seven o'clock in the morning. There was a heavy mist; the haar which rolls in from the sea and drenches Aberdeenshire most mornings in autumn. It was market day and the farmer had fat cattle to go.

The haar had deadened the sound of the lorry until it was almost on the young stags as they grazed the roadside. Almost at once it was upon them from out of the mist. The headlights blazed and the diesel engine roared as the driver changed down to take the corner into the farm close. Ten deer bolted. Nine cleared the fence and landed in the potato field but the tenth didn't make it. He didn't see the wire fence on top of the dyke. He was catapulted back almost under the wheels of the lorry. He bounced to his feet and made a perfect clearance of the fence at the other side of the road, into the barley and away.

And so it was that though nine of the deer were recaptured one was never seen again. He looked hard for his companions but always in the wrong places - and when the haar lifted and the sun came out, the loneliness and all the light and space drove Fergus, as we'll call him, into a thick pine wood to sleep the day away.

Fergus might have spent his life at that wood for there was plenty of cover and a choice of fertile fields all around for a variety of foraging. Neeps, he liked them for there had been none at Little Ardo, grass and aftermath of barley with plenty of heads that had been missed - that was somehow better than the bruised stuff he'd been fed in the bull's box. But it was almost October and the rutting season and he must keep looking though he had no idea for what.

There were even other deer in the wood but they were Roe and though he had no difficulty chasing off the bucks, he had the same effect on the does. And they didn't turn him on anyway.

So Fergus kept moving on and on until one day he awoke beside the wide river - and there it was, the unmistakable smell of the peat and the heather and the real deer from the hill. It was coming down the great river and it awakened in the young stag the ill-remembered feeling of home in the hills with his mother as a calf.

He started to walk and graze and walk up stream, led on by the scents of home and as the days passed and the smell grew stronger, Fergus felt more strongly the joy and aggression which nature brings to young stags each October.

The fertile lowland plains gave way to thinner land and poorer fields. Then to green hills and finally to birch woods and heather. Fergus was home, not that he knew until one day he heard the crack crack of antlers and smelt the stronger deer smell close at hand. He'd stumbled on a large herd of red deer.

He ran towards them full of inarticulate joy.

But that was not the happy ending. Ten months in a bull's box on a lowland farm doesn't tell a young buck how to behave in the rutting season. And a trip from lowland Aberdeenshire to the height of the Grampians is not good training for a fight. Fergus's mad joyful rush was taken as a threat by the monarch of the Glen who turned his four hundredweight and eighteen pointed antlers on the challenger. Poor Fergus didn't stand a chance nor did he know when to flee.

CHAPTER FIFTEEN

# The Paris Show

"NO I'M not coming to the Show, John Stephen. I know fine that we're supposed to be here for the Agricultural Show and I also know fine that's the only reason we can get our holiday through the books, but you'll not catch me spending my 'Springtime in Paris' looking at coos and tractors," said the farmer's wife.

In truth it wasn't springtime. The Paris Agricultural Show is held in January. It's just far enough after Smithfield and Christmas though, to make it an attractive four-day jaunt. So with the marvellous summer of 1984 behind him and a monster tax bill looming for any of the profit he hadn't spent by April the 6th, John Stephen had decided to join the ever-expanding number of British farmers who found it imperative to the successful management of their few paternal acres to visit Paris for the Show.

Now, if John's principal reasons for going to the Paris Show were that so many of his pals were going, that he liked good food even if it cost £20 a plate and that he had a pathological hatred of paying tax, Avril's motivation was altogether different. If John's conversation could be summed up as 'neeps and strae', plus the necessity of voting conservative, irrespective of what they had done next, Avril was an altogether more cultured flower.

For Mrs John Stephen was a leading light in the Tarves Literary Society and had once nearly got Sir Mortimer Wheeler there to tell them about the stones of Vienna (or was it the stones of Venice, she could never quite remember), and of course she was a member of the

Haddo House Choral and Operatic Society... and not just one of those who hangs about and you'd see with their photo in the papers when there were visiting dignitaries, for Avril was a pretty good singer. It was at the 'Choral' that she'd been introduced to opera. They'd started with Gilbert and Sullivan where Avril had been one of the three little maids from the Mikado's school and she'd understudied Casilda in The Gondoliers. They'd also done some of the classical operas like The Barber of Seville and La Traviata. She had thrilled at the passion and strength of those great melodies and she was determined not to miss the opera in Paris. In fact Avril could hardly wait and had been dreaming secretly for weeks of humming quietly along in the cavernous resonance that would envelop their seats in the Dress Circle at the Paris Opera House.

So on their first day in Paris it was: "Off you go to your Agricultural Show. I'm off to see the Sorbonne."

In fact, they were both a bit disappointed. Avril found that the Sorbonne was much like any big, old, dirty and crowded university, and John didn't really think the Agricultural Show was much better than Smithfield or the Winter Fair in Edinburgh, except that there were rather fewer of John's pals in Paris, or at least they were more difficult to find in the crowds.

However, when they met up again in the evening, John had a treat in store. If his wife had come to Paris for Culture rather than Agriculture, then he'd show her some. He had booked a table for two, nearly at the window, for dinner at Maxime's... overlooking the Seine and across to the Cathedral of Notre Dame, all floodlit and magical.

Now a menu in French can be bad enough at home but at Maxime's they're not used to translating, or at least the Stephen's weren't about to try them, so John had the Compote de Pigeon Bourgeois and Avril had the Cotelettes de Lapins Ecossais. They saw the joke when they realised they'd had pigeon stew and rabbit fritters. "Here we are in Paris paying a fortune for a diet we put down as vermin at home and wouldn't dream of eating unless we had to." Mind you, the laughing had to stop when the bill had been translated from eleven hundred francs to a hundred and three pounds... for a poacher's diet for two.

For all it had been delicious and that John was not a poor man, he was taken aback. It was when he was still reeling from that blow but mellowed by the lion's share of the two bottles of Maxime's claret, that John Stephen agreed that the next evening they would go to the Paris Opera. "At least it'll be a cheaper night out", he thought.

And so it was that John and Avril Stephen learned some more truths about recreation in Paris.

Even John couldn't help being impressed by the sheer scale of the Paris Opera House; the great pillars and statues, the grand sweep of the stairs leading up to the boxes, and the sheer voluptuous majesty of the auditorium. "It's some change from the one and sixpenny cuddlies at Montrose", John whispered.

That was after the ordeal of choosing the seats. They soon discovered that there was no Dress Circle at the Paris Opera House so they tried for the Orchestra Stalls. Further still from the one and sixpence cuddlies at Montrose, the best seats at the Paris Opera House were forty pounds a head (though John thought that maybe 'head' wasn't the right word), but luckily they were all taken. The cheapest seats, on the other hand, were only six pounds but they were something called 'sans visability'. Well, even John's French was good enough to make him suspicious about those... could it really be that they had the hard neck to sell you a seat without a view? Naturally Avril was deputed to ask a silly question like that.

Indeed it really was so... six pounds a seat from which you couldn't see the stage. Eventually, and after much heart-searching, the Stephens settled, in partial disbelief, for seats costing thirteen pounds and boasting 'partial visibility', which turned out to mean that if you wanted to see the stage you had to stand up.

They were the back pair in a box for six on the third tier. They were shown to those seats by a very chic lady. "If this was Montrose", John thought, "she'd have had a fag hanging out of her mouth, be called an usherette and sell ice cream at the interval."

But this was Paris. Her job done, the chic one smiled at John with just a hint of menace. "Service," she said.

"Oh, a drink. This is some use now," John thought to himself, "Aye, I'll have a beer, what about you dear?"

"Non, non," said the chic one, "SERVICE!" and she rubbed her thumb and forefinger together like a graduate of the Fagan School of Charm.

The Stephens were indeed far from home. John gave the usherette a handful of change and was pleased to see the back of her.

The opera the Stephens had stumbled on was a very modern thing called 'Wozzec' and it was a big disappointment. Not, you understand to John, who was quite unburdened by high expectations of the evening, but poor Avril could forget her dream of singing along to familiar choruses. It wasn't so much that the choruses weren't familiar as that there weren't any choruses at all. Indeed to the ear tutored at the Haddo House Choral Society there were no tunes even, let alone choruses.

To make matters worse the story, which would have been hard enough to follow with the Stephen's O-level French, was in German. There seemed to be a lot of soldiers posing rather than singing. They were clearly the chorus - the ones who, in the operas that Avril was used to, played the parts of gracious courtiers. Certainly this lot would have been much more convincing as courtiers than as soldiers in Wozzec. They were done up in neat-fitting grey tights and tee-shirts and that most revealing of uniforms demonstrated very clearly how unusual it is to find a trained operatic voice in a body that's fit for combat.

Indeed the fat bellies hanging out of the ridiculous tights were the only thing John enjoyed about Wozzec for he was bored out of his mind. And yet he couldn't let Avril know it. He knew better than that. When they were watching the telly at home, she was at his throat if he as much as sighed in boredom. So the poor farmer sat and suffered and watched his watch. Fifteen minutes gone... he looked around the auditorium. It was almost full. The seats cost an average of about twenty-five pounds each. The place held about three thousand people. "My God," he thought, "that's seventy-five thousand pounds a night to watch this rubbish. Oh no, still only sixteen minutes gone." John could hold his breath for a minute, so he tried that... seventeen minutes gone. Avril still looked intent. John decided to try to work out which of the grey figures on the stage was Wozzec himself. He failed, but at least it took him to eighteen minutes.

And John took to telling himself stories like the one about the two highlanders discussing the new minister:

"Oh a capture for the parish," said Hamish.

"Teed yes," said Johnny Ban, "there's a man could haff been a doctor or a lawyer or a teacher even. Anything he could haff been. He's no much of a minister mind, but you can't haff everything." Still only nineteen minutes gone.

Try another story. The one about the lorry driver who was asked in the early days of motorised road transport to take the load of turnips to London. That was a good one because it could take as long as you liked:

It was a fair undertaking for Wullie, who had never been further than Aberdeen with cattle for the mart, but he set off with a will in his old Albion. He drove and he drove and he drove until he came to a great metropolis. Just to be sure, he stopped at the first person he saw and asked if this was London.

"Dinna be daft," came the reply, "this is only Montrose."

So Wullie drove and drove and drove till he came to another great metropolis which again wasn't London but was in fact Arbroath... John spun the story out as far as he could by making Wullie stop and enquire for London at every town he could think of on the way to London, and even spent a few more valueless seconds by sending the load of neeps on several detours to take in towns which weren't on any sensible route to the capital.

Despite John's endeavours, the neeps arrived in London all too soon. Wullie stopped a policeman on points duty and asked him:

"Hey min, is this London?"

"Yes it is, mate, Piccadilly Circus."

"Thank God for that," said Wullie, "Far are ye needin this neeps?"

"Oh my God, still only twenty minutes gone... hold your breath for another minute."

The excruciating boredom, and the not even being able to squirm in his seat in case Avril noticed, went on and on. Eventually forty minutes did pass but there was no interval. At fifty minutes, John made up his mind that when the interval did come, he would be man enough to tell Avril that he wasn't going to sit through any more. But he needn't have bothered. At fifty-six minutes, amid much noise but still no discernable tune, the whole thing stopped. There had been no interval and the Stephens had been so far out of their depth that they hadn't even noticed the three acts being run together. The seventy-five thousand pound happening had happened and John had made it through his darkest night.

John Stephen never discussed Wozzec or the Paris Opera with his wife but she was strangely quiet when they left the theatre. They had walked a bit down the street when she took his arm:

"I think I'll come with you to the Show tomorrow, John," she said.

# CHAPTER SIXTEEN

# *The Turra Coo*

THIS IS the true and celebrated story of a Shorthorn Cross Ayrshire milking cow from a medium sized farm in Aberdeenshire which, in the days before the First World War, was known throughout the length and breadth of Britain and was even written about in the London Times.

It all started with the National Health Insurance Act of 1912. Up till that time all health care had to be funded privately and the poor, the unemployed and unemployable - well they had to rely on private charity or none. The Liberal government of the day and their leader (who had the distinct disadvantage, as far as his critics were concerned, of being Welsh), David Lloyd George, prepared to introduce certain benefits like ten shillings a week for the sick. Now no-one was objecting to that but what went down very badly with the hardy and Tory people of Aberdeenshire was the proposal to pay for that by a levy of 7 pence per employee, 3d to be paid by the masters and 4d per week by the man. That was nine shillings and sixpence out of the hard-won earnings of maybe £25 pounds for a half year.

Opposition was widespread and furious. The farmers burned an effigy of Lloyd George in the square at Inverurie. The doctors in Aberdeen threatened to strike against what they rightly saw as the thin end of a wedge that would separate commerce and health in their dealings with their patients. And in 1911 and 1912 Aberdeen, Ellon and Turriff saw demonstrations of men and masters against the Insurance Act.

Now all this passion threw up two heroes - or rather, one hero and one heroine. She was the 'fite coo', a quite unremarkable dairy cow. And the hero was her truly remarkable master, Robert Paterson of the fine farm of Lendrum near Turriff.

It would be easy to characterise Paterson as a typical peasant farmer who didn't believe in anything but his own pocket, but that would be inaccurate. He was an educated man for a start, he even studied agriculture at college in Canada. He was a progressive farmer, being among the first to put down concrete in his byres and to use steam for sterilising equipment. And he was a self-made man who rose from helping his mother with her dairy in Turriff to owning land on seven estates, including Lendrum's 250 good second-class acres. There were ten men working on Lendrum and there were many tales of Paterson's kindness to them. I'll give you one illustration only:

One of the Lendrum men broke his fee (or six month's contract) and left. That was a bad crime at the time and this man was rewarded with the loss of his new job and his mother's health. When he went back to Lendrum to seek re-engagement, Paterson told him: "I'll take you back, laddie, for your mother's sake."

Well, well, Robert Paterson refused to pay his threepence per employee per week on the grounds that they didn't want him to and went to court for arrears of £3.19/=. He was fined £15 and would have gone to jail but for the fact that some of his farmer friends paid the fine for him.

But that still left the £3.19/= plus expenses to pay to the National Health Commissioners and, as Paterson still refused to pay, a white dairy cow was, as the legal jargon has it, poinded. It was to be sold at Turriff Market Cross to pay Robert Paterson's debt. That was the first of the Turra Coo.

That was to have been the end of the matter but the authorities reckoned without the solidarity of the Aberdeenshire community. It was agreed among all the farmers and dealers of the area that no-one would bid for her, so that way the Commissioners would be stuck with a worthless cow - and Paterson planned his own act of defiance. On the side of the cow he painted a derision at Lloyd George:

# Lloyd George and the cow
# from Lendrum to Leeks

and on its rump a facsimile of the hated insurance stamp.

Old photos of the great event show the Square at Turriff a sea of bonnets as they waited breathlessly for the sale by Macduff auctioneer Sam Gordon. They glanced occasionally at the tall, erect and quite stunningly handsome Robert Paterson, at forty-six and at the height of his powers and about to claim national fame, or notoriety.

The Turra Coo arrived, led on the halter by a loon. It was 1913 so what happened next happened a long time ago, but was something like this: Sam Gordon was making nothing of rouping the cow - despite being down below a pound he couldn't get a bid. The mood of the crowd was of hysteria. Derisive laughter wasn't far from anger.

Then at once a crowd of young farm servants arrived on bicycles. Someone let off a firework. The crowd surged forward, someone cut the coo's halter and she bolted, taking no further part in that day's action.

But everybody else did.

The police, who were outnumbered by several hundred to one, were pelted with stones, potatoes, rotten fruit and eggs and horse dung from the road and nearby stables. And poor Sam Gordon, who was only trying to turn a bit of honest commission and who hadn't looked forward to the sale, who had hated the look of that enormous crowd and who had taken to his heels at the very first sight of trouble, finished an absolutely miserable day besieged in Cheyne's stable several streets away.

That was the Insurance Riot at Turriff which lasted until nightfall.

And the fite coo? Well, she ran and she ran on the road home to Lendrum until she was caught at the farm of Mill Moss. And milkman John Mair from Lendrum got a new halter on her and had her home in time for milking.

73

But that wasn't the end of the saga of the Turra Coo, for the Commissioners weren't finished yet. And the next time the fite coo returned to Lendrum, she was accompanied by her own pipe band.

The Commissioners would take her to Aberdeen and raise the money there to pay Robert Paterson's arrears, plus expenses. And so it was that a week after the Turriff Riots, the fite coo was once again on her travels. She was led the four miles to Auchterless station where she was loaded, like any ordinary beast, in one of the cattle wagons.

I don't suppose the Turra Coo would have minded the fact that she was leaving the fine farm on Lendrum's hill, and the view over the Vale of Ythan and down to Fyvie, but she would fairly have missed the second-cross Shorthorn calf that appears with her in some of the photographs. But that was nothing to the excitement of the next few days.

When she got to Aberdeen and disembarked at Kittybrewster Station, there was almost as big a crowd as there'd been at her abortive sale at Turriff. The cow was greeted by cheers - and the officer in charge of her by a certain amount of good-humoured abuse.

She was to be sold at Kittybrewster Mart and was led round there, followed by the eager, excitable crowd. But when they got to the gates of the mart, things started to go wrong for the Sheriff's Officer, and farmer power proved itself far stronger than it has ever done since. For the gates remained shut and the Mart manager told the Commissioners that farm workers were never ill, never unemployed, and shouldn't have to pay this tax; and in any event Kittybrewster wouldn't sell the coo.

This was greeted by a great cheering from the ever-growing sea of cloth bonnets. Ah well, they would try the Central Mart, but no luck there either and the Belmont wouldn't open its gates either. There wasn't a mart in Aberdeen would take the coo.

But the Sheriff's Officers weren't to be beaten and they knew that while the farmers could organise a boycott of the sale at Turriff, there were just too many potential buyers in Aberdeen. There were butchers, processors, dealers from the south and from

Ireland, who would certainly bid for the Turra Coo if there was any chance of a bargain. And there were indeed plenty of vultures in the town that day because they knew most of the regular buyers would not bid on principle.

So the coo was marched down to Crail's stables near the station and taken inside to be sold, with the doors barred to the huge and potentially volatile crowd. So most of Robert Paterson's supporters were excluded from the sale and from seeing who was bidding, but one supporter did get in.

He was a farmer/dealer from Gamrie. He took on the vultures and bought the coo for the princely sum of £7. So the Commissioners got their money, the crowds had their fun, and Paterson made his protest. But the story didn't end there.

The coo went home to Gamrie, where a public subscription was taken up among the farmers of that district and when the fund reached £7, arrangements were made to return the coo to Lendrum. This was done at a ceremony in the little park they use for machinery roups in the middle of Turriff. There were about five thousand people there when, to the strains of the town band playing "See the conquering hero comes", the fite coo was led into the parkie by James Davidson of Longside.

And as a last stab at the tyranny of Lloyd George she had painted on her side: Free - divn't ye wish ye were me!

After the presentation and the speeches, the crowd and the band led the Turra Coo home to Lendrum in triumph.

That was the end of the politics for the white coo. But not for Robert Paterson. It was a dreadful shock for him, a deeply religious man, when at twenty minutes into the sabbath, the Turriff police arrived at his door with a summons for causing the riot in Turriff. He tried to declare the summons illegal, as it had been issued on a Sunday, but he and seven others were tried in Aberdeen before a packed courthouse and with daily reports in the *London Times*. And when Robert Paterson was acquitted, the Turriff band was out again and leading a tumultuous reception with 'Here the Conquering Hero Comes' again as he stepped down off the train at Auchterless station.

And the coo?

She died on the farm six uneventful years later, in 1920. She was buried in a corner of the cornyard and fifty-one years later a memorial was raised to her and Robert Paterson on the roadside at Lendrum. I see it often as I drive from Gight to Turriff.

# CHAPTER SEVENTEEN

# *Oceans o' Muck*

ANDREW AND Kate Kelman had been happy enough with one another though they were long through the first flush of passion that had produced their four children in their first five years of marriage. There had been some hard times then, as the four fought their way to adulthood and tested the very limits of parental patience. Indeed in Andrew's case those limits weren't that wide, and there had been difficult times for Kate as her husband's attempts to explain right and wrong to her sons had degenerated into hopeless beatings. She'd even thought of taking them away at one time - but where do you go?

And anyway she knew she had a good man at heart and that it would all come right - and so it did. The children grew up and left home. The girls went to college and middle-class jobs. The boys went to highly paid labouring jobs on the oilrigs and though Andrew could fine have been doing with a hand on the farm, in truth, he was glad to see the back of them.

So the Kelmans settled into a middle-age of friendly indifference. He looked after his 100 suckler cows on his 120 good acres while she looked after the house and the garden, and remembered the children's birthdays.

Now, you could see that after the children had left, that was a lopsided division of labour. Without the children, the house and garden were much easier, but the farming was a bit more difficult when the supply of go-fors and herders dried up.

And farming, which had never been easy, was to become more and more difficult through the 1980s as the priority in agricultural policy moved away from more food to saving the taxpayers' money, and interest rates went through the roof. As anyone who has travelled that road will understand, Andrew Kelman grew dourer and dourer as he tried to maintain his

income by running harder and harder each year. Meanwhile Kate, as the presenter of two modest meals for two each day, was happy in her kitchen and as guardian of her sweetpeas.

But all that was to change. It started when Kate was displeased with her blackcurrants in 1983. It had been a good summer... enough rain and plenty of sun and yet Kate didn't have a crop. More muck was the verdict and there was no shortage of muck at Little Milton for, as Andrew often said, his hundred cows and their calves produced 'oceans of muck'.

But it's one thing having oceans of muck in the midden and it's quite another thing getting a busy farmer who has a hundred and one things to do, to deliver it to the garden. Kate asked for a 'loadie of muck to the garden', demanded 'a load of muck for my garden', girned for 'my muck to your garden', and then sulked until one day Andrew could no longer stand it.

"Right, I'll gie her muck," he said, yoked a cart and filled the yard with load after load of steaming manure.

By the time Andrew was finished, the garden was fair full. It was quite a mess really. The muck was dumped on top of the gooseberries, and the rasps had a huge load on either side of the row Kate had taken a first with at last year's Flower Show, so that some of the canes were broken with the weight and the rest peeped out no more than a couple of feet above the sea of fertility, like some exotic sea of dwarf canes. And to get into her garden to survey that scene, Kate had to climb over the cart-loads Andrew hadn't managed to get through the gate.

It didn't even enter Kate's head to protest that her man had overdone it. She had asked for muck and she had got it and she was damned if she would lose face by admitting that she could fine have been doing with less. She set to work, and though it cost her backache and blisters, though she had to dig up the drying green and though it took three weeks of her life, Kate eventually got it all turned under somewhere. The blackcurrant bushes looked a bit funny though, for the ground had risen a good nine inches and buried that much of their stems.

"Thanks for the muck, Andrew," she said, "there'll fairly be blackcurrants next year."

And so there were. And the potatoes she'd put in where the lawn had been were the best the gardener had ever seen and as for the leeks, well, they were so big that even one would have done the broth for a steam mill.

But what was she to do with all this garden produce? Half an acre of burgeoning fertility was more than two of the most ardent vegetarians could possibly eat and the Kelmans were hardly that. Depending as they did on their calf production business, they could hardly be that. In fact Andrew saw vegetarians as a positive menace. She could sell vegetables, Kate supposed, but she would have no real hope of competing with the professional market gardeners in the rest of the Clyde valley with their big acreages and mechanisation. However she got the seeds of an idea when she went over to Haddington to the funeral of a cousin of hers.

Andrew had grudged the day off and was in, if anything, a worse mood than usual. He was farming away as he went and seeing nothing but ill in what he saw: this farmer would never get calves till he bought a decent bull; and that flock of sheep would fatten as well on a tarmac road they were so short of grass. Kate got her idea when they passed a sign at the end of a farm road. It read:

## FOR SALE
### Organic Farm Vegetables

"Oh, that's vegetables grown without manure and half-eaten by slugs because they dinna spray them." Andrew explained.

Kate said nothing. She had never liked using pest cides, for she reckoned that anything that killed animals - eve a insects or snails - likely wouldn't do human beings much good either. And her vegetables weren't manured with anything but good honest muck.

"Oh yes," she decided, "my vegetables are certainly organic."

So, despite Andrew's sneers, up went the sign at the end of Little Milton's road, and Kate was in business.

To her amazement her venture was an instant success, especially when the cars came streaming out of Glasgow at the weekend. There were some days when there was hardly enough room in the garden for the customers, let alone enough vegetables for them. Kate decided all this demand was because her prices were too low. So they were, for, modest lady that she had been, she had thought she would have to be cheaper than the shops. But not a bit of it. Kate doubled her prices until she was almost charging as much as Marks and Spencers and still she couldn't keep up with the demand.

It was after the dreadful summer of 1985 that Kate asked Andrew for another half acre to grow more organic vegetables. Well that did it. "Good God woman, whar hae ye been? Dae ye no ken whit like a year it's been? My calves are doon forty pounds a piece, straw's costing me eight pound a bale and you want an extra half acre to play at gairdens - well you can forget it."

But the farmer didn't forget it. He made fun of the market gardener and her slug-infested lettuce and wormy carrots, and made all his pals at the mart laugh and laugh.

And Kate didn't forget it either for, though Andrew didn't realise it, she was far beyond being discouraged by a few sneers. In fact she managed to rent a whole acre from a neighbour. She got a contractor to plough in oceans of muck in her new ground, and with teams of ladies to do manual weeding, de-slugging ladies and packaging ladies she was soon supplying the local private school, several hotels and four fruit shops in Glasgow with Kate Kelman's Kountry-Fresh Organic Range.

Of course all that success wasn't down to Kate's genius alone. There were two big swings in public taste that made it all possible. First, there was a swing away from eating all the meat you could afford, to eating more and more vegetables. That didn't please Andrew because it was bad for his business, but what infuriated him beyond measure, was that the trend was promoted by two groups of scientists financed by the taxpayer at great expense, who had opined that meat eating was bad for your heart... as though scientists would know anything about it. And then there was the swing towards 'natural foods', whatever that meant. That seemed to start with a report that showed the amount of pesticides we were eating, especially on imported vegetables. What a boost for the natural food brigade. And then there were all those European rules banning growth-promoting hormones and antibiotics, which made meat production so much dearer; there had been no word of that when they had that referendum on their damned E.E.C.. Andrew Kelman fairly thought the world would be a better place without all these interfering do-gooders... and as for that wifie, tennis player Nina Navritawhatever-she's-cried, she's just a bitch trying to put folk off eating meat.

But however little Andrew liked it, while his beef produc- tion enterprise was under considerable pressure, the organic vegetable trade was on the up and up. The great breakthrough for Kate came when George Smith of Graham's, the Glasgow Fruit Market traders, decided to start on his own with a pitch dealing only in organic produce. That meant Kate could concentrate on production and leave distribution to the specialists.

And it was George Smith who persuaded Kate that really she

wasn't fully organic. For that, and to earn the right to use the triangular organic logo, you had to leave the ground fallow for three years and have it tested to make sure that there was no trace of chemicals.

In that case she'd need two more acres - and, as luck would have it, a croft came on the market, just up the road.

But Kate wasn't the only one who wanted to buy that.

Andrew's calf-production enterprise was struggling and like farmers the world over, he saw the solution as lying in expansion. The extra eight cows he could keep if only he could buy that croft might just do it, he thought, and so did the local college adviser. But, unlike Kate, Andrew's hurdle was money. After the disasters of the 1980s the banker was on his back. So the farmer plucked up his courage - but not his humility - and went to the market gardener for the money.

"I'll need about eight thousand pounds tae buy Upper Milton to keep a few more cows," he said.

"Oh no you don't, Andrew Kelman. I've expansion plans of my own. De ye no ken Smiths are crying out for mair organic veg. and that the new organic co-op's setting up at Thornhill? I can't spare the money for ten acres so that you can play at fairmies."

Andrew was beside himself with rage but he wasn't finished.

"Right," he says, "I'll charge you fifteen pound a load for yer muck. Where'll you be then? eh? eh? It's just my muck that's got you on. What have you to say about that? eh? well?"

"Oh aye, Andrew, I was going to speak to you about that," said the organic market gardener, "I won't be needing your muck any more. You see, I'm going fully organic next year. That means I canna use your muck because you use artificial manure on your parks, so your cattle are nae organic-fed. I'm paying fifteen pounds a load for my muck next year all right, Andrew, but nae to you."

## CHAPTER EIGHTEEN

# Jimmy Sutherland

THIS IS the true story of the time the railway tried to buy over Jimmy Sutherland's bus company.

I'm sure Jimmy's mother would never have imagined that day when she set him up with a pony and two-wheeled spring cart when the boy was just twelve years old. That was back in 1876 at the start of the Great Depression, but it's a funny thing: no matter how hard work is to come by or how deep the depression, there's always somebody with enough drive to find a job and do it well.

And so it was with Jimmy Sutherland. His first work was carting sand from the shore to the fishermen's cottages about Peterhead. They used to spread it on their earthen kitchen floors. And the spring cart, the sheltie and the boy were so quick that there was plenty of time to diversify and sand was soon being carted to the farmers round about for grit to their hens.

The business grew and prospered, for Jimmy Sutherland could not only get the job done but he could get his customers to pay. In less than two years the sheltie was replaced by a grey Clydesdale and the spring cart gave way to a proper four-wheeled lorry. Then Jimmy Sutherland could cart gravel and stones from the quarries for the roads and for the railway which would one day have the cheek to try to buy him out.

Jimmy Sutherland could shift everything and in the fullness of time he did but the first real breakthrough came when he went into fish. He had already moved some white fish in short hauls around the harbour at Peterhead. But in 1882 he won the contract to haul fish to the town from the neighbouring villages of Burnhaven and Buchanhaven. Then men had to be hired and more horses bought and by the time he was twenty, the laddie that had started with the sheltie and the spring cart was employing a dozen men.

From fish, Sutherland moved into carting people. Cabs for weddings, brakes for meeting the train at Boddam and ferrying them to Peterhead and an ambulance to take folk from the Blue Toon to the Infirmary in Aberdeen.

Now all that enterprise and all that growing was achieved in the Great Depression, so as things started to get going again at the turn of the century and in the run up to the First World War, Sutherlands really took-off. By 1914, fully two hundred and fifty horse were being yoked every day. Branches had been set up in Great Yarmouth and Lowestoft, and Jimmy Sutherland sent as many as sixty horses south by rail each year to those ports at the height of the herring season. That was an important trade in its day, for the Sutherland horses didn't come back at the end of the season... they stayed to be the backbone of the farming industry on the great wheat farms of East Anglia.

Sutherland's first horseless carriage was a traction engine. It had been a wonder in its time no doubt, but its impact was insignificant compared with the Seldon motor lorry that was bought in 1915. In 1916 Sutherland took the seats from his horse-drawn charabancs and fitted them to his lorry to take the school bairns to their picnics, and by 1920 Sutherlands were running regular daily bus services to Aberdeen. And it was then that Jimmy Sutherland first came into conflict with the railway.

The services started with a bus fare of fifteen shillings return but the intense competition that ensued cut the fare to as little as three shillings, and at that the railway just couldn't compete.

And so it was that the directors of the great North British Railway met the laddie from Peterhead who had started with a sheltie and a spring cart and tried to buy him out.

The protagonists had made a rare contrast: thick-set grey-haired open-faced Jimmy Sutherland, who hadn't forsaken the well-polished leather boots, faced the pinstripes and old school ties of Edinburgh.

Whatever they expected, they soon found that Jimmy Sutherland was no pushover. Try as they might they could not get him to sell. He had men who deserved his loyalty. And what would he do with all the money they were offering as he had plenty for his needs already. "I can only wear ae sark at a time, gentlemen," he told them. And despite a long day's inducement, the men from the railway had to give up. Sutherland's Transport just wasn't for sale at any price.

The meeting was breaking up - somewhat dejectedly, when Jimmy Sutherland lent over to the chairman of the North British Railway Company and said:

"Well now, it seems a pity to waste a whole day's work without a deal of some kind." The chairman's eyes lit up. Was this the break-through?

"How much are you needing for your railway?" said Jimmy Sutherland.

# CHAPTER NINETEEN

# *The Tak Doon*

JAMES McCONVILLE (Junior) was a very important man in the really not very important village of Rhynie in Aberdeenshire. Why he chose to call himself 'James McConville (Junior)' instead of 'Jimmy Mack' like anyone else, no-one was quite sure. After all, his father hadn't been James McConville (Senior), even if you ignored the rumours. For James's dad was Willie McConville. He'd been a jolly, feckless chap, who sadly had died young. And maybe it was an attempt to live up to his father that could explain the 'Junior' bit, for James had to listen to the praises of his father all his life - "Oh, you'll never be the man your father was".

And that cruel prophecy was spot on, for James McConville (Junior) was not a nice person. It wasn't that you could just pin anything bad on him, mind you. It was just his attitude. No-one else ever did anything right except by accident, he always knew best and he could hardly say 'Good morning' without making it sound like it was more than you deserved. James McConville was a pig. You know, when he went down to the Christmas Fatstock Show at Perth each year he was away for three mornings and he cancelled his newspaper. *He* wouldn't be there so he cancelled it. He never thought that his wife, who didn't get to Perth, might like a read when he was away. And worse than that even, was the time he nearly took the wife to London. It wasn't like James to bother about the wife but they were newly married at the time, so perhaps that's why he did intend that year to take the wife with him to Smithfield to the Show. At any rate, he went to see the banker and told him he'd be needing a hundred pounds because he was taking the wife to Smithfield. That was all right of course but what scandalised the village was that James was back a couple of days later asking if he couldn't make it two hundred pounds on the grounds that the wife had taken ill and couldn't come with him after all.

Now for all that, and for all his talking loudly through other people's speeches, James McConville (Junior) was one of those people who command the sort of place in the community which many mistake for respect. When important people like the laird came to the village to open something or when the MP came at election time, it was always James McConville (Junior) who proposed the vote of thanks.

He was well-off of course - how could he help it with the best farm in Rhynie and the money his wife had brought to their marriage. It certainly was nothing to do with the sweat of McConville's brow. For he was lazy too, and that, with his inordinate appetite for food and drink, meant that he was asked to join the Board of Aberdeen and Northern Marts. James McConville (Junior) was a big man and still growing.

The impending board membership was an event which called for a new suit, so James went to see Harry Forbes, the tailor in Rhynie. He chose the best cloth, of course, but was totally bowled over by the asking price:

"That'll be £24.10s.6d." said the tailor.

"Fit?" said James McConville (Junior), "you're a bandit Harry Forbes, that's far ower muckle for a suit. Good god, man, I'd need the title deed for your shop for money like that."

"Well, James," said the tailor, "you know, it's the amount of cloth involved and the work of tailoring the waistcoat and jacket round your stomach."

Well there were more words but, to cut a long story short, James took his trade elsewhere and landed at Hewitt's, the 'Tailor of Distinction', in Aberdeen. Now it was well known that Lord Aberdeen's gamekeepers got their suits at Hewitt's, so

James was sure of a good suit, though he was nervous about the price in so grand an establishment. Could £24.10.6. really be the price of a good suit these days? Well, well, if it was, it was better to be fleeced in Aberdeen than to lose face in Rhynie. When the measurements had been taken and the estimate arrived, James braced himself.

"That will be eleven guineas exactly," said the manager of Hewitt's.

You could have blown James McConville (Junior) over with a sigh. "But that's most reasonable. How do you do it? I mean, all the cloth and the tailoring round my stomach and well, frankly, I went to the tailor in Rhynie - not that I would actually shop in such a place, you understand, but just to get an idea. And that bandit Harry Forbes tried to charge me £24.10s.6d. He said it would take so much cloth because I'm such a big man. How can you do it for eleven guineas?"

"Ah well, Mr McConville, it's like this: you may be a big man in Rhynie, but in Aberdeen you're just one of the crowd."

# CHAPTER TWENTY

# *Glenprosen*

"CHARLIE MIN? Polly's needin ye tae fase ower een o yer funcy bulls til wir coo." It was my neighbour Sandy Taylor. He explained that their house cow which should have calved six months ago, had turned out not in calf once again. The AI man had attended her regularly every three weeks for nearly a year and a half but to no effect. "Ach," said Sandy, "the AI's aright when it works but it's a damned expense when it disna."

I was pleased to be asked and looked forward to striking a blow for traditional methods of reproduction.

Nothing but the best would do so I chose Glenprosen. He'd already been champion at Turriff show and his mother had been champion at the Royal Highland and Ingliston. Surely that would be 'funcy' enough.

I felt it was only right that Glenprosen should do his courting in his best coat, so I washed him thoroughly with plenty of Lux, gave him a blow-dry and combed his hair up with some three-in-one oil so that he glistened in the sun.

We were a magnificent sight as we set off to walk the mile or so to the croft. Not since I was a boy have I wanted to have a dog but I got something of the joy of walking one as I swung along the road with my fourteen hundredweight doggie on the end of its halter. Perhaps we could make a career of this. After all it was only putting the breeding of farm animals back a few years. My father had had a friend who used to tour the countryside with his stud boar to see to all the sows in the district. And then there were the stags, the stallions who toured round the farms seeing to the thousands of Clydesdale mares who used to provide most of the power on Scotland's farms. And they do say that it wasn't just the stags that got work though it was long before my time so it's not for me to say. But there had been plenty of work for the great stallion Methlick Again. He had been so busy that he had to be taken off the road in the middle of one season. He was exhausted but there's no word of whether it was the walking between jobs or the work itself that did it.

Oh yes. Glenprosen and I could easily take the road together for a season.

As we passed the other crofts on the way, nervous neighbours peeped out, for news of our journey had gone before us. Children were kept in lest they be gored by Charlie Allan and his "funcy bull".

As we rounded the last corner we saw Sandy and Polly standing in the neat little close. And there was Daisy, a fine Shorthorn-cross-Ayrshire cow of some ten summers, rinking enthusiastically with a little black and white heifer she had for company. Things looked right for Glenprosen to start earning his corn.

It was decided that Patricia, the little heifer, would be better out of it. It would simplify matters for the young bull. Daisy was taken into the little court and left to Glenprosen's eager courtship.

Sandy, Polly and I retired and left them to it. We would go to the house for a business dram. We would easily know if Glenprosen had completed the contract because, if he had, Daisy's tail would be sticking out.

It wasn't long before we were sneaking back to see how things were progressing. I'm afraid they weren't. Glenprosen had not the slightest idea of what he was there for except that his hormones were telling him that it was a pretty auspicious occasion. He was excited, you could see that, but he didn't know what to do about it. And for all that Daisy had already had ten calves, they were all by AI and she had not been through this particular door either. So there they stood back to back looking distinctly bemused.

Polly, who had been a keen student of nature, was confident that time would find a way and we retired for another business dram.

But if time would have healed we lost patience with waiting for it. We decided to put the two of them outside to the field to rejoin Patricia. Perhaps a menage a trois would help.

It did. Being back with her pal seemed to settle Daisy and the added dimension fairly cheered Glenprosen up. Soon Daisy's tail was sticking out proudly.

It was a really fine day and we had another business dram to celebrate and then another just because we had acquired a taste for it.

Then I caught my bull and waved goodbye and set off for home. Glenprosen gave never a backward glance and there was an assurance about his step as we swung rhythmically along. As the sun beat down I put my arm over the great wide back, and resting my head on the soft flank, I floated along. I could have slept there on the road.

CHAPTER TWENTY-ONE

# To Book a Seat on the Buchan Line

IT HAS been a source of great wonder and no little annoyance to the people of Aberdeenshire that the BBC should see fit to do a television series on Great Little Railways and not have included the Buchan Line. That was one of the later additions to the great network which in Victoria's reign brought together town and town, and town and country, and brought anywhere in the country to within one day's travel of everywhere else.

The Buchan Line ran from Aberdeen to Fraserburgh through Formartine and Buchan, some of Scotland's most diligent rural heartland. And it was a lifeline.

There were two main cargoes: cattle and people. Both stores and fat cattle were loaded and unloaded at the big markets like Kittybrewster, Ellon and Maud and at little halts like Arnage. The cattle were driven on foot the rest of the way along narrow unmade roads to and from the farms - distances of up to ten miles. Then there were people: ladies from the country going to Fraserburgh or Aberdeen to the shops; farmers going to the marts; students from the countryside going up to the fancy schools in Aberdeen, to the University or the Agriculture College.

And as the Buchan line went its way through the country collecting and distributing its people and its cattle, it cut itself a nitch in the affection, indeed love, of the Aberdonian - not least because of the way the tinyness of the railway carriage threw people of alien cultures and classes together. Before the railways the ladies of Aberdeen would never have been in social contact with the peasant farmers of Buchan.

The social mixing was not always a success. One banker from the South, on his way to see a really big debt at Peterhead, arrived lateish for the train in Aberdeen. He entered a compartment which was almost full of farmers all smelling of the land and smoking bogey roll - the toughest tobacco ever to enter a meerschaum or a clay cuttie.

"Excuse me gentlemen, is that seat taken?" It obviously wasn't, so the banker interpreted the lack of reply as assent and sat down. Not a word was spoken until the train reached the junction where the branch went off to Peterhead.

"Well gentlemen, this is where I get off. It's been so nice meeting you, thank you for your company, and good day."

Again not a word was spoken by the farmers until, after the banker had gone, one turned to another and said, "an affa bugger to news that," and his friends agreed without actually saying anything.

It would, though, be a mistake to think that the lack of small talk means the Aberdeenshire farmers are inarticulate or are pushovers. Take the solicitor who was going back from Fraserburgh to London. It was about time for luncheon so he decided to go along to the dining car. There was no-one in the compartment but just in case anyone joined the train at any of the many stations on the Buchan line, he left his bowler hat to claim his nice corner seat by the window.

That worked fine until the train arrived at Ellon. It was Friday and the carriage was invaded by farmers set for the mart at Aberdeen. The first man into the compartment saw the hat, fancied the seat in the corner, lobbed the bowler into the luggage rack and sat down.

By the time the solicitor came back the compartment was blue with the smoke of Bogey-roll and bluer still with descriptions of the weather. But the air wasn't so thick that he couldn't see his seat had been taken. He entered confidently.

93

"Excuse me, my man," he said, "that's my seat you know."

"Oh aye," said the farmer, moving his pipe to the other side of his mouth, "How's that?"

"Well goodness me, didn't you notice? I booked that seat with my bowler hat there."

"Ah well, mannie," said the farmer, " ye may as well ken - it's erses that books seats on the Buchan line."

# CHAPTER TWENTY-TWO

# *James Stephen*

JAMES STEPHEN was a substantial and a very good farmer. He was a big but not heavy man with sharper features than is common among the farmers of lower Donside. Passionately interested in agriculture of course he had an intense, restless manner in conversation and was always in a hurry. When he would meet his fellow members of the Aberdeen and District Milk Marketing Board it would be "Aye, aye. Yes, how are the coos doing?" and he'd be off to speak to somebody else without waiting for the reply. He knew he'd have heard if the cows had got foot-and-mouth disease and he hadn't the time to waste on the inevitable non-news that they were "fine" or even "grand" which he knew full well would only reflect the impression the speaker wished to convey and would have nothing whatever to do with the cows' performance.

Strange to relate though, this fast man had one very slow eccentricity and one which was quite out of keeping with his restless pursuit of all that was progressive. Long after all his big farmer friends had been converted to the internal combustion engine as their principal means of transport, James Stephen kept his gig, the two-wheeled light carriage which had carried generations of his forefathers swaying and clattering about their business.

No one asked James why it was that he chose ten miles an hour rather than fifty, so I don't know why. But there are those who say that it was an affair of the heart with his old mare Bess. But that gives the wrong impression. For though Bess was no longer young... James had already taken nine good foals out of her... the impression she gave was of vitality rather than age as, ears pricked, head pecking like a black woodpecker, shoes clipping into the Inverurie turnpike, she tore her master home to Conglass. I don't know how good Bess was really, but James Stephen thought her a wonder, and for the purposes of this story that's all that matters.

Well now, on this particular day James and Bess were bowling along on the road from Inverurie up to Chapel o' Garioch to look at a park of stots. James was busy planning the work for the next day or two and keeping an eye on his neighbours crops so Bess was, as was not unusual, doing the steering.

It was a lovely day and they weren't the only ones who were enjoying it. The Miss Birnies were out for a run too and they had stopped for a breath of air and a touch of the sun but mostly to feast their eyes on the brand-new, bright-red Morris Minor. It was the new model with the two seats and the two extra roofless seats that were revealed when you opened the boot. The Miss Birnies were bursting with the pride of ownership which had been secured for the remarkable price of £100.

And wonderful as Bess may have been, with James's attention fully occupied with a field of turnips, she went too close to the Morris Minor. The crash of the gig's inside wheel on bodywork so alarmed Bess that she gave a terrified breenge forward and ended up in the ditch at the other side of the road, with the gig coupit.

James, who was thrown clear, was unhurt but he wouldn't have noticed anyway for his concern was all for Bess who had taken a considerable dunt and was, in her panic, compounding the danger by thrashing a leg against the gig in her attempts to rise.

With an effort, eventually James got her lowsed, whereupon she struggled to her feet and, with the distraught farmer holding desperately on to the reins, she reared and plunged, ears forward and nostrils flared in terror.

The Miss Birnies, meanwhile, were unimpressed with all

this drama. What about their beautiful new car? In truth the damage wasn't substantial, but you know how it is with a new car: once it is bashed or even scratched it will never be quite the same again. "Oh look at this dent here," said Penn, "And look, there's another scratch on the mudguard," cried Lill. And their mood wasn't improved when, with James hauling and Bess plunging, the mare somehow landed with her feet in over the boot seats. "Oh look what he's done now," cried Lill, "Look at my lovely upholstery."

But James Stephen could not have cared less about their upholstery, he was far too concerned for his mare. It was quite tricky but he did eventually get Bess to do one more rear and get her front feet back onto the ground where she stood, blowing hard and shivering, always on the point of taking off again.

"Fine Bess, fine Bess," said James, as, keeping the reins tight to give her assurance, he felt fearfully and tentatively down his sheltie's legs for the break which would mean she'd have to be put down. "Fine Bess, fine Bess. There's a fine lass. Woa lass, woa lass." He started with the two front legs which he was fairly sure would be OK. And then the right hind leg which had some nasty scratches on it. "Fine Bess, fine lass..." that seemed to be alright too. He left the left hind leg till last. It had been uppermost as Bess lay with the gig on top of her in the ditch and it was the left hind leg that she had thrashed against the carriage as she tried desperately to rise. Now she stood with it half forward with no weight on it. There were more than scratches here and what James really feared was the weal that was developing fast on that shin.

"Oh dear, what a mess," said Penn and,

"Oh no, here's some more scratches on the wing," said Lill "It's just not fair."

"Some folk might watch where they are going." said Penn.

Finally the apprehension for his mare got the better of James. "Oh hud yer tongue you twa. Maister Morris is makin a car every minute, but search the world you'll never get anither horse like Bess." But luckily he didn't have to. The shin was whole and in a matter of weeks Bess was back in harness.

Having satisfied himself that his horse was going to be

alright, James took more interest in the Miss Birnies' treasure. He paid for the damage to the car which Barclay, Ross and Hutchison were able to return to a condition almost as good as new. But, for all he acknowledged that the accident had been his fault, James Stephen never quite forgave the Miss Birnies for their priorities.

# CHAPTER TWENTY-THREE

# *English Rose*

ALBERT AND Rose left civilisation in the South-east of England with only a little trepidation. He had got a plumb job as Head Cattleman at the Mains of Northam, one of the biggest dairy farms in the country. Things might have been easier for them for they arrived just before the terrible storms of January 1984.

The young couple had just two weeks of normal weather before the storm broke. That weather had been bad enough but it suited the young cattleman alright; he was too busy getting the farm properly redd up to notice much. There was plenty to do and he worked day and night at it. But Rose wasn't so pleased. She was separated from all her pals and from her mother. The old lady would have known what to do with the rambling old farmhouse they were living in. That had been part of another place that had been added to the Mains and it wasn't what she had been used to.

It wouldn't come clean for all that her duster poked and pried and the central-heating system had about as much effect as a candle in a cold store. And it didn't help that when Albert came home each night he was so tired that he was no more use than a hot-water bottle when it was time to climb the creaking stairs to bed.

So when the January storms came the couple were hardly best prepared. And it wasn't the calm Surrey snow that you watched falling gently by the window and landing wetly on the ground. This was furious horizontal snow whipped up by gales of

99

up to a hundred miles an hour. In the middle of the first night the electricity went off. That meant that when they got up at five the next morning there was no light to put on. They didn't even have a candle and of course there was nothing to cook on. So it was a cold and hungry young cattleman who stumbled out to plunge through the snow-drifts along the half mile or so to the steading.

When dawn broke around half past eight the young wife saw

the extent of the snows; a level fall of some fifteen inches had been blown up into drifts of up to fifteen feet - and some said they were even deeper than that. From the bedroom window, through a patch she was able to melt in the ice, she surveyed the white wilderness which her new home had become. Telephone and power lines six inches thick with ice looked like giant strings of spaghetti lying haphazardly between bent and broken poles and the only sign of life was from a flock of rooks casting about for food in a world which had been robbed of all its familiar landmarks.

The poor English Rose wandered round her great, cold and empty farmhouse - for the furniture from the cottage in the South was quite lost in her new home - and whenever she entered another room her hand automatically switched on the light, and each time nothing happened and she was startled. Well at least she could listen to the radio - what would they be saying about the storms on the news - 'Oh no, that's worked by electricity too'.

The central-heating was off, of course, but at least she could have a coal fire. She would fill the coal bucket. But when she made it to the place where the coal-shed had been, there was only a snowdrift. With her bare hands Rose burrowed into the snow until she came to the roofless coal, half filled her bucket, and rushed back into the house frozen and crying.

There was to be a lot more crying. For the electricity was off for a fortnight, and that meant poor Rose had no cooker and no water save for melted snow.

On the other hand the weather suited Albert fine. He enjoyed the challenge of the snow and the new dimension it brought to his work. For the first time his job became one of survival... get them fed, get them milked and try all you can to get the milk away to the creamery and find somewhere to store what can't get away. Niceties like feeding to yield and calving intervals could wait for less exciting times. The new baillie even managed to shoot a hungry pheasant - a thing he would never have dared to do in Surrey.

But Albert dreaded coming home for his meals. He hated them anyway, cold meat out of tins with bread and cold milk - though one of the other wives did eventually show Rose how to boil a kettle on the coal fire, so after that there was hot tea - but mostly he hated to see his poor wife so out of her depth and so miserable.

By the tenth day Albert was ready to quit. For all it was by far the best paid job he'd ever had and, with over 400 cattle and three other men under him, one of the most prestigious he was ever likely to get as a baillie, his wife's sanity came first. So when he went home that night he took her in his arms and shared her conviction that that cruel land had beaten them and that they must return to the South. But though Albert didn't notice it, an odd thing happened. When her tears had dried, Rose's face had set in determination.

Albert worked the next day with a heavy heart for he had

already come to love his beasts and that wild country and he was loath to leave. He went home that night resolved to make their plans for a retreat to a more familiar world. But when he arrived the young baillie was met by a smiling wife, and it was a smile he had not seen before, one of triumph:

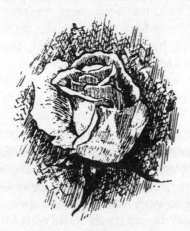

"I've won," she said "and we're staying here." She led him into the front room. It was aflicker with candles and the fire, banked up with coal, roasted the room with a fierce glow. And it wasn't just the room that was roasting. For there in front of the fire, balanced on the fire-dogs and spitted on the poker, was the pheasant Albert had shot, crackling brown and ready for the plate.

Rose maybe hadn't beaten the storm but she had taken the first step and they were staying at the Mains of Northam.

## CHAPTER TWENTY-FOUR

# Alford Show

ANGUS AND Jeannie MacWilliam had all that they ever wanted and that included one another. They'd had the farm to themselves since Auld Angus had died and he'd done that in decent time when they were still young enough to enjoy working the place for themselves.

There were only 60 acres of Kinharradie farm but they were pretty busy acres, as busy as any in the Vale of Alford. Their main business was the rearing of calves from the dairies round about - though they were weaned onto turnips and silage - and each year

Angus brought as many as 300 five-hundredweight Black-Hereford heifers to the Alford mart. He enjoyed the admiration of his fellows as much as he enjoyed the cheque and both were considerable, for he made a good job of his cattle.

They were a good team really, for Jeannie kept hens for the house and kept a clean house as well as rearing calves. And Angus milked the cow and saw to the outside work as well as taking a job at the tatties or as relief dairy cattleman at some of the big farms round about.

They didn't spend much - no Mediterranean cruises - or even a weekend at Stonehaven for Angus and Jeannie - but Angus did have one annual breakout - to Alford Show. He'd always taken a heifer to Alford Show and usually got a prize, though Black-Herefords were hardly showy beasts. For weeks before, Jeannie would hear roars of abuse and anguish and indignant 'moos' from the byre as Angus halter-broke, trained and finally groomed and polished up his entry for that year's show.

And that was all very well but on the show day, after the judging, Angus would invariably retire to the beer tent - and the judging was usually over by 10 am. So by the time Angus had shown his beast in the grand parade of livestock at 1 pm, he'd got a taste for it and he went back to the tent for the afternoon. He could be guaranteed to be in a gey state by night.

Well Jeannie didn't really mind that. He was a hard-working man and a good husband, and he would surely get a break-out once a year. But she drew the line after the year when he got so drunk that he forgot to bring his heifer home - and she'd won second prize in her class.

There would be no more of that - and that was the end of it. In future he could go to Alford Show if he liked, but there was to be no nonsense about taking a beast. Mind you, that suited Angus fine, for the beast had only been an excuse in the first place.

Now if this idyllic couple were less than idyllic in any way it would be in the relationship between Angus and his sister-in-law. He could see that she was a worthy enough woman but he just could not stand Jeannie's sister. Whenever she'd come to visit he'd get an excuse to go outside or sit in his big armchair with a face like a foot, hunched and scowling into the fire.

It was so bad that Jeannie's sister got to visiting only once a year - when she knew Angus would be away at the Alford Show.

Well now, on this occasion the sisters had been so engrossed in their chatter that Aggie had missed the train. What would she do?

"Oh you'll be alright. Angus'll be so fu when he comes home, he'll never notice you're there. And I'll get you up to the early train before he's wakened."

Although there was only one bed, Aggie agreed to stay. And when Angus came home blind drunk he rumbled into bed before his muddled brain registered anything amiss. But gradually he became aware that something was amiss - or he thought so.

"Hey mother, there's six feet in this bed."

"Oh shut up, Angus, ye're drunk."

"I ken I'm drunk but there's ower mony feet in this bed."

"There's only four Angus, go to sleep."

"There's six feet in this bed mother, and I'm gettin up tae coont them."

Angus humphed himself up and staggered round to the bottom of the bed, pulled up the covers, "One, two, three, four. Hmm. Oh aye, mother you're right enough. There's only four."

He tottered round into bed and put out the light.

"Oh and mother, remind me tae wash ma feet in the mornin, will ye?"

# CHAPTER TWENTY-FIVE

# Ernie Wilson

THIS IS the true story of a young horseman who left his native Aberdeenshire during the first world war and went off to America to make his fortune. I say it's a true story but of course it happened a long time ago and Ernie's dead now so the exact and detailed truth isn't that easy to come by, but if I've made any mistakes I don't think I've done any violence to the spirit of his story.

The worst part had been leaving Mary Shewan behind. She was in service in the next parish. But they were betrothed and they both knew that though the parting might be long, and would certainly seem it, it could never be permanent and that a parting there had to be.

Ernie had made the decision one Sunday when he was still a loon at Balquhindachy; the biggest farm in the parish of Methlick. His father was the grieve there and Ernie had eight brothers and sisters. It had been a difficult spring like so many of them in Scotland's North-east and in an effort to catch up, Ernie had spent fourteen hours on the Saturday holding on to the two Clydesdales while his father sowed grass seed... the precious seed upon which the somewhat fragile prosperity of rural Aberdeenshire depended. Well, the next day, father and son were walking home from church, their Sunday best getting a gentle soaking from the little rain. They were walking up the Doctor's Brae on the first of their three miles to Balquhindachy, when the farmer drew up in his gig; "Jump up grieve. There's room for you but I doot the loon'l hae tae walk."

And it was as he trudged home alone in the rain that young Ernie Wilson decided that he would leave the North-east. He just wasn't going to work for folk like that. He'd heard tell of the great opportunities for a hard-working youth in America. The school-boy decided there and then that as soon as he could he'd go to America and he'd fairly show them hard work.

Mary Shewan's father, too, was a grieve. He ran things at the Mains of Schivas. She'd been brought up by a god-fearing mother who had schooled her thoroughly in the old-fashioned virtues of thrift and housecraft... Mary could turn out a girdle scone which, with raspberry jam, would bring the sap to the driest mouth... and though she was loath to lose him even temporarily, she was all for her lad getting on. Mary too saw their future as being far from the North-east.

Young Ernie Wilson was seventeen and had made it to second horseman at the Mains of Schivas (fine handy that, for seeing Mary) when he saw his chance. The local mart got a big contract to send Shorthorn cattle to Canada. They advertised for a cattleman to accompany them. The wages would be negligible but it was the chance young Wilson had been waiting for.

Mind you he wasn't alone in that, for, as another young ploughman who was in it told me, the queue for that job stretched 'about a mile doon the street' as eager young men sought the chance to escape from a Europe which was entering its fourth year of a devastating war and was stifled by class barriers.

Some said it was favouritism because his father was grieve at the great farm of Balquhindachy, but when the lucky name was read out it was "Ernest Wilson".

Mary Shewan didn't let her lad see her cry. She held on until he had gone, and then only her mother knew, for the sixteen year old lassie maintained the bearing in which she had been schooled.

Ernie Wilson had never been further South than Stonehaven but, in what seemed like no time, he had disembarked his cattle in Montreal and was ready to set forth. It was the year 1917 and he'd heard of the great things being done in Detroit by Henry

Ford and others in the new motor car industry. Ernie was determined to go there and get himself as big a slice of that action as he could. He was in the right continent now but only in Canada and it was there that young Wilson had it brought firmly home to him just how far from Buchan he now was and just how far he still had to go. For Montreal was French-speaking and when he asked "Far div ye get the train tae Detroit?" the young Scots ploughman was met with blank stares. At length he saw a tall red-headed man striding along. Surely this would be a fellow Scot. Ernie summoned up his best English. "Excuse me but where de ye get the train for Detroit?" he asked.

The tall red-headed man didn't even look round. "Frightfully sorry, don't speak a word of French." he said and hurried off.

But despite that and other set-backs, Ernie did make it to Detroit where he joined the thousands of young hopefuls, attracted from all over the world, queueing for work and a chance to join the new expanding motor car industry.

But rapidly though that industry was expanding, the queue was long and it was very hard to get to the front. Soon starvation forced Ernie to take a job as a stoker... that was the hardest work and so the highest pay he could get. But Ernie wasn't like so many of the other immigrants. That money wasn't for the night life but for night school... for Ernie was determined to train as an engineer and build cars.

It took Ernie the best part of a valuable year to get his foot in the door of the automobile industry and when he did it was little more than a toe-hold. It was a start though; as a labourer to a machine-operator at Fords. It was a poorly enough paid job - less than he'd been getting as a stoker - but the determined teenager from Scotland wasn't long in establishing himself. He called it a stroke of luck; but was it? Fords had been on one of their periodic efficiency drives and an engineering discussion involving revolutions-per-second and centrifugal force and one thing and another had got up on the lathe to which Ernie Wilson was labouring. Neither the operator nor the engineers knew off-hand how to do the calculation. But the labourer did because he'd been studying that very subject at night-school the previous evening.

That earned Ernie Wilson his own lathe and a living wage... the sort of wage a Scotsman could save off.

The studies and the saving continued and soon the young man had another stroke of what you could call luck. Having been through the Scottish system of public school education, Ernie had a head start on his fellow immigrants and his American colleagues. And that proved decisive when one of the senior executives at Fords - quite by accident - saw one of the young Scot's timesheets. He asked the line-manager whose was the beautiful copperplate handwriting. The lathe-operator was sent for and so impressed the executive with his character, presence and determination that he was offered a college training as an engineer and a Ford staff salary to go with it.

And that was what Ernie Wilson had been waiting for, working for and saving for. And he wasn't the only one. Back in Scotland a kitchie-deem at Schivas House had been waiting for three years for her ploughman laddie to send word for her to join him in America. Mary Shewan was still only nineteen when she kissed her mother for what she knew might well be the last time and left with pride and a third class ticket for her new life. She can hardly have known then of the style in which she was to return.

Mary's welcome to America was enthusiastic and loving but hardly lavish. Ernie had bought himself a plot of land on the outskirts of town... a fine site with a view of developing Detroit. One day a fine home would stand there, but there was no money for that yet and the young couple started their married life in a tiny log cabin Ernie had built in the little spare time he had between studying at college and working at Fords. Mary liked her new home fine but she was glad her mother couldn't see it for the old lady would certainly have called it a 'timmer sheddie'.

But even her mother would have had to admit that it was clean and it was cosy and it would only be for a while for the young couple were still ambitious and were on their way.

Ernie continued with his studies and with working at Fords when he could. And it was when he'd been working very late on some problem or other and had been walking home in the rain that one of the directors of the company passed in his limousine. He stopped and offered Ernie a lift. That was fine for it was fairly a night for a lift.

When they got to the parting of the ways the lad was all for being dropped at the corner but the director of the great Ford Motor Company would have none of it.

"Not at all. I'll take you to your door... night like this."

Ernie couldn't help noticing the contrast with the time in Aberdeenshire when the farmer had left him to walk home in the rain on the excuse that one more would be too much for the horse. But Ernie Wilson had come to a land where all Jock Tamson's bairns got a chance. So when he was home the ploughman was bold enough to ask the director of the Ford Motor Company in for a cup of tea.

The great man was intrigued by the young man's earnest conversation and by the sight of the log cabin, and to Ernie's horror he accepted.

He needn't have worried for his guest was captivated by what he saw. For Mary had all the wood scoured white and all the metal shining just as she'd had in the kitchen of the big house back in Scotland. And of course he'd never tasted a bannock or a girdle scone and raspberry jam before, so he just didn't have a chance. With all that and Mary's good looks, good manners and bearing he was quite captivated.

So much impressed was he with what the young couple had achieved and their hopes and plans for the future that when he took his leave, the director of the great Ford Motor Company said to the 21 year-old ploughman and his twenty year-old servant lass from Scotland.

"You're the sort of folks that should get on in life and I'm going to see that you do."

And so he did.

From that day onwards, Ernie Wilson's progress up through the ranks at Fords was steady and sure. And it wasn't just a matter of patronage, though there is no doubt that had helped, for Wilson turned out to be a brilliant electrical engineer just when automation was starting to invade the factory floor. And on Ford's production lines there was endless scope for his talents and energy - though not all his ideas were an instant success.

The day came when Wilson was in charge of a whole shift on one of the lines. His latest innovation was to have all the holes in the bodywork bored automatically instead of each assembler boring his own when he needed them. Now the new system worked beautifully on Ernie's shift but on the 4 am till noon shift there was always something going wrong: progress was always being held up because there was a hole which wasn't quite in the right place. The delays were costing the company a lot of money and the great Henry Ford himself was not amused.

The inventor was sent for.

"Godammit Wilson, these ideas of yours are all very well but they've either to work or not... sometimes is no damned good to me."

Things looked bleak for our man, but the two agreed to make a formal study of the problem and at five o'clock the next morning Henry Ford and Ernie Wilson found that somebody on the morning shift was indeed doing something he shouldn't, and Ernie and his latest innovation won a reprieve.

But things were never to be the same for Ernie Wilson, for that incident and the production that problem had cost Fords, taught Henry Ford a lesson. He saw that the company were car-

111

makers, not experimenters with electrical control systems. Brilliant as Ernie's ideas were, it was just too risky to have them developed on Ford's production lines with all the disruption which would inevitably be entailed. That was a job for a separate company which would work in electronics and sell the results to Fords.

And that, with the aid of the Ford millions, was the start of Wilson Automation, the company which over the years saved Fords hundreds of millions of dollars and made the second horseman from Mains of Schivas a multi-millionaire.

So, like Scots the world over, Ernie Wilson and Mary Shewan were able to show the rest how it was done. By Ernie's genius and both of their hard work, thrift and patience they were to get out of life all that they had hoped for and worked for... including a return in triumph to Scotland.

Ernie went to America in a cattle boat and Mary went the cheapest way she could. But when they came back it was on the Queen Mary. And they didn't have to hire a car or hail a cab when they docked at Southampton. For when they came, as latterly they did each year, the Wilsons brought their own custom-built Ford with them. I never saw the car but I asked one of Ernie's fellow horsemen about it.

"Oh," he said, "I canna mind what it was ca'ed but it was that big that when the front wheels were going round the corner to the Fyvie road the back wheels were still on the bridge at Methlick."

Ernie travelled all over the old country in this monster and even took it on a tour of Ireland. It was in the west of that country that he stopped at a filling station and said to the attendant:

"Just fill her up...she'll take about forty-five but just fill her up."

Now it was a hand-operated pump and this was considerably in advance of the usual order at Ballyhurly. The lad's face was soon a bright red as he pumped away furiously. Eventually the pumping stopped and the desperate operator appeared at the driver's window,

"Excuse me sir," he said, "but would you mind switching off your engine a minute please. I don't think I'm winning here."

112

In this mobile advertisement for hard won success, Ernie Wilson drove up the Doctor's Brae and every year told Mary of the exact spot where the farmer of Balquhindachy had left him to walk home that rainy day before the Great War. Then up to Balquhindachy to see the little cottar-house which he had shared with his parents and eight siblings. Then over to Schivas House to see again where Mary had been able to watch how the other half lived while in service - and all the while conscious that if they had wanted to they could have bought out the lot - but they never did.

# CHAPTER TWENTY-SIX

# The Laird and the Loon

THIS IS one of those stories which is very difficult to get at because of its place in history. It is true, without a doubt, but I'm afraid the exact nature of that truth is in considerable doubt. It happened a long time ago and was memorable enough to survive as a folk tale but was never important enough to appear in the history books.

The principals were the Laird of Esslemont, John Wolrige Gordon and a seventeen year old fee'd loon from the Mains of Esslemont. They must have made a fine contrast.

Robbie Taylor was a chirpy, wiry loon and willing. A bright spark who would tackle anything and who often needed his smile to get him out of trouble. He'd left school at thirteen and his ambition was to become a horseman before he got married and filled a cottar house with bairns.

John Wolrige Gordon was quite another kettle of fish. Apart from having the wealth of Esslemont behind him he was a Sandhurst-trained professional soldier with the rank of colonel. He had served in Ireland and later in the Boer war and had spent a good deal of his civilian time in the more desirable parts of southern England. He was a civilised and refined sort of gentleman.

When he became Laird of Esslemont on the death of his father in 1906, John Wolrige Gordon brought to the estate the same sort of discipline as that upon which he had insisted in the army. Robbie Taylor would have done his best if he had to, and done it cheerily enough; Colonel John must have everything done correctly and to time. In that last he was most particular. Everything must be done to the minute, and that did mean everything and everybody - with one exception.

The soldier had married late and he could hardly have married better save for her appalling sense of time. She would wander in for lunch at half past two but, to the amazement of everyone else, she was never chided in any way. They say it was because he loved her so much that Colonel John let his wife have her way with time. It may even be that he knew that she didn't have much of it. For Isabel died in 1910 in giving the laird a son and heir. It is said that Colonel John never smiled again. Not, that is, until 1914. When the telegram came, summoning him to rejoin his regiment, he was upstairs in a flash and down again in five minutes, wearing his uniform of colonel in the Argyll and Sutherland Highlanders. They couldn't see his face then for smiles.

Our story though took place in the non-smiling time.

In 1910 there was a great harvest home concert and dance in the school hall at Esslemont. That celebration was known locally as a 'Meal and Ale' after the unique and nutritious mixture of beer and oatmeal which serves at once as the basic food and drink for the occasion. It's a sort of poor man's Atholl brose though no doubt there had been some of that mixture of whisky and honey as well.

As was his wont at such public occasions, Robbie Taylor would do a party piece and it was in his choice of that that he fell out with Colonel Wolrige Gordon. For the song that the lad chose was a ribald ballad concerning one of the laird's ancestors and which showed him in an unflattering light.

Charles Napier Gordon, a renowned shot and fisherman dedicated to emptying the river Ythan, was a bachelor all his days, not because he didn't like women but because he preferred the challenge of making an endless stream of women happy to the much easier and more predictable path of making one woman miserable.

Anyway Robbie Taylor sang the old ballad that relates the

time in the middle of the 19th century when "Charlie" Napier
Gordon "ran awa wi the weaver quine". I've never heard the song
and I'm afraid those who have are dying off fast. All I've got are
two snatches:

> *The weaver bade at Rora*
> *Two miles past Longside.*

She had been walking in Esslemont when she accepted, most
unwisely, a lift in the laird's gig.

> *Awa they sped like ony kyards*
> *The horse clicked up his heels*
> *They hadna gone a hunner yards*
> *When aff cam baith the wheels.*

The spice on the ballad lay in what happened next. It is
related that the laird took advantage of the unfortunate accident.
As they were thrown conveniently onto the grass he made amo-
rous advances to the weaver, though that bit of the ballad relating
to the success or otherwise of his suit is among that which is lost.
One version of what actually happened survives in the local
folklore. It says that, while the laird was pursuing his advances
the couple were come upon by some of the weaver's kinfolk who
took a dim view of the proceedings and gave the laird a hiding.
There is even a suggestion that the weavers had sprung a trap on
the laird, knobbling the gig and supplying the temptress to
facilitate blackmail.

But the truth of what happened in the original incident is not
important to our story. The important thing is that in 1910 the
current laird took exception to the song being sung at a public
occasion and called Robbie Taylor to book. Indeed, according to
local folklore, the laird took the loon to court in Aberdeen and had
him fined, though whether that was for breach of the peace or
obscenity, or whether it was really an action for damages, I cannot
say but one way or the other the boy was left short of five pounds,
and those were the days when a haflin could work two months for
a fiver.

So Robbie Taylor was in sombre mood as he trundled back
to Esslemont in the third class compartment of the train to Peterhead. "Still," he thought, "at least I've still got my job."

116

The laird too was coming home on the Buchan line, though, of course, he was travelling first class. There could be no communication between the two when the train was moving for there were no corridors. But at Logierieve station, the last one before home, Robbie was astonished when the laird appeared at the door of the third class compartment.

The laird opened the door and entered. Room was made for him in the crowded compartment. He sat opposite the boy and eyed him up through the smoke of bogey-roll and the other gentler odours of country folk returning from market day in Aberdeen. Eventually he spoke, "They tell me that song of yours is not a bad song Taylor, but you know I've never heard it. If you'll sing it to me and to our good friends here, I'll give you five pounds for your trouble."

It was not what the loon had expected and he was taken by surprise at the laird's matter-of-fact and even kindly tone. The loon had sung often in public but he'd never been paid anything for it, never mind five pounds.

They say Robbie sang his heart out that day on the train and that there was hardly a dry eye in the compartment. They even say the laird was seen dabbing at a tear, though I wouldn't like to vouch for that.

The song finished as the train drew into Esslemont station. The laird stood up, drew out his purse and counted out five gold sovereigns and held them out to the boy "And, Robert Taylor," he said, "If you ever seek to make fun of the the Lairds of Esslemont again, you'll ask my permission first."

If ever such an occasion arose, I'm sure that he did.

CHAPTER TWENTY-SEVEN

# Red Rob Macdonald

THIS STORY is inspired (if that's the word) by Mel Gibson's creative attitude to Scottish History.

Like all countries which are blessed with large and protective neighbours, Scotland had many heroes even before the days of Ally McCoist. There was William Wallace who held back the might of England almost single handed on the narrow Bridge of Stirling, Rob Roy Macgregor who leapt sixty feet to freedom at Peterculter, Flora Macdonald who smuggled Prince Charlie across the sea to Skye and away to France and the exciseman Macpherson who they were so keen to hang that when they knew the reprieve was coming they put the clocks forward an hour rather than miss his hanging.

None of those may be properly understood but they are all well known. This story is about a little known and totally unsung member of Scotland's Hall of Heroes.

Red Rob Macdonald terrorised the loyalist forces throughout the length and breadth of Scotland in the latter half of the eighteenth century. He specialised in ambush and usually worked alone. He would creep up behind a column of redcoats, despatch one or two and then disappear into Scotland's ubiquitous mist, often without even alerting the rest of the troops.

Red Rob had no political agenda, just a strategy of indiscriminate violence and tactics of unpredictability. For Rob was driven by a wild hatred of the English and their German kings.

But if there was one class he detested above all else it was the loyalist Scots. And top of that class, he hated General Colin Dewar, the Black Fox of Argyll.

Red Rob had a most remarkable presence. One of the widest men that ever lived, his chest measured sixty-three inches when it was expanded, and it was nearly always expanded for he was a proud man. He wasn't tall and with his flaming red hair he had something of the appearance of one of those old fashioned nightlight candles. He wore his kilt in the manner of one who could find nowhere else to put it. And under that kilt strained two of the strongest legs in Scotland. The leather thongs that held on the remains of his soft hide shoes seemed in constant danger from the heaving nut brown calves.

Well now, it was on a fine day in late autumn that Black Fox and his regiment of redcoats were riding through the Glen of Appin when suddenly, on top of a steep bank, not three hundred yards from them, appeared the horrid figure of Red Rob, dancing up and down and screaming abuse; "G'wa hame to yer masters in England ye treacherous blasphemer," he screamed at the Black Fox amid considerable and imaginative blasphemy of his own.

"Corporal, take two men and go and despatch that fellow," said the general. The three redcoats set off up the hill to do poor Red Rob in. But just as they reached the summit Rob jumped over the brow and out of sight. When the three redcoats followed him there came a great roaring and a clash of steel followed by three mortal shrieks, and then silence. A minute later Red Rob reappeared.

"You'll need to do better than that Black Fox," he shouted, "Three redcoats is just about what I need for ma breakfast."

Colonel Dewar was displeased. "Hmmmm, let me see. It's half past eleven... let's stop for elevenses. Sergeant, take your platoon and get rid of the vermin on yonder bank." Black Fox settled to his tea and sandwiches.

But when the platoon were reaching the top of the little hill, Red Rob again jumped over the horizon. When the platoon followed, the crash and cries of battle could be heard quite clearly in the Glen of Appin.

After half an hour all again fell silent until Red Rob appeared, his great chest heaving and the blood lust in his eye.

"Next," he roared.

"Brigadier, take your brigade up after that fellow and I'd rather like to talk to him so bring him to me alive, if you would. Meanwhile, it's time for luncheon. The rest of us will dine."

So off the brigade set up the hill. The same thing happened again and the sounds of battle did rather spoil Black Fox's luncheon.

Soon it was spoiling his afternoon tea. Still the clash of steel and the cries of death rolled down the hillside to the remains of the regiment. The mists of evening started to drift down the hillside and still the battle raged.

Then they heard a single cry. It was coming closer. Someone was coming down the hillside. At last out of the mist they could see the figure of a stumbling redcoat, covered in blood and dirt, his sword and musket gone and bleeding horribly from a wound in his neck. He staggered up to the Black Fox... "It was terrible sir. Don't send any more men. Save the remains of the regiment. It's a trap. There's two of them."

## CHAPTER TWENTY-EIGHT

# It'll Mak nae Difference

THIS IS about the father of the hero of chapter twenty-five. Ernie Wilson's father was an important man in Aberdeenshire being grieve at one of the biggest and best farms in the county. And while his son became a multi-millionaire in America, Jake Wilson remained on the land of his forefathers and was proud to do so though his wage would never have exceeded 65 pounds for the half year.

Jake Wilson was a tall, well set up man. When he was young, his thick strong black hair, alert, restless face whose jewels were two striking hazel eyes, and his broad shoulders and body without an ounce of surplus on it, gave him an aura of athletic power. But our stories of Ernie Wilson's dad concern him in later life. The hazel eyes had earned the reputation of missing nothing, his greying though bushy mouser had added authority to the handsome face and his physical presence and years of being a grieve gave him the certainty that only years of command can give.

And Wilson's command wasn't just a case of shouting orders and kicking backsides; he was an expert in man-management as the following example illustrates.

It was 1924 and the man who had to be managed was the third horseman at Balquhindachy. James Low was himself to

121

become one of the legendary grieves of North-east Scotland and at twenty years old he was impatient to get on to that position of authority. He had already put the other lads at Baldies' noses out of joint by winning the affection of Isabella Christie, the best, bonniest and most agreeable of the three deems about the place and was set to marry her at the term. And in his work the third was forever pushing, pushing to show how good he was. He was never satisfied unless his furrow was better turned than the next man's or that his harness were on first at yoking time... aye and remember that was no mean ambition for the third horseman as the foreman had, as a matter of etiquette, to start first and you couldn't be seen to hurry.

Now Low's aggressive attitude to his work wasn't all good as far as the grieve was concerned. Certainly it meant that he got a high standard of work from his third, but a grieve has more to think of than such short-term advantage. Jake Wilson believed in the concept of the 'happy ship' and to achieve that the odd high-flyer had to have his wings clipped.

The grieve and the aspiring grieve were quite a contrast really; Wilson's classical good looks and bearing were matched against Low's traditional Aberdeenshire shape... short legs and a long strong body with magnificent shoulders, and topped by a rather sharp-featured face. And it was more than their physique and twenty-odd years that separated the two for they had a different approach to things. When James Low was to become a grieve he would be known to take his jacket off to his men to assert his authority. But Jake Wilson had a cannier way.

Of all the men at Balquhindachy who felt the weight of Low's push to prove himself, naturally the second horseman had most to put up with. Alec Stott was a good man and willing but no match for James Low who would always try to get in an extra load, or an extra drill, or be finished first, whenever they worked together which as second and third was the normal way. Now to take the edge off this, Wilson set about trying, where possible, to keep the two apart so that invidious comparisons would be impossible. He would put Stott to ca' neeps and Low to the plough in the morning and reverse the procedure in the afternoon.

It was a good idea but not good enough.

"Aye Stott," said Low at yoking time," foo mony straik did ye manage this mornin than?"

"Five," said Stott defiantly.

No more was said, but at five o'clock Low was coming through the close having emptied a load in the neepshed, when he was met by the grieve.

"Foo mony loads is that ye've hame, Jimmy?"

"Five," said the third, "but there's plenty o' time for anither een afore lowsin time."

"Na, na. That's plenty neeps hame for the day. Lowse your horse the noo and we'll ging doon the Quarry road and cut some breem or lowsin time," said the grieve, who hated cutting broom just as much as the third horseman did, but something had to be done to protect poor Stott and to hold young Low back.

Of course there was more to Jake Wilson's stewardship at Balquhindachy than keeping his men in order. He had to see that the seed was in in good time, that harvest was taken when it might be, that the cattle and sheep were treated when they were sick and sold when they were fat. He had to be a stockman and a husbandman, and by all accounts he was very good at both but in a somewhat traditional way. He wasn't one of those who favoured change for change's sake and rushed into every new idea that came out. He'd fairly make progress, but he regarded innovation with suitable scepticism and preferred to let other farms act as guinea pigs.

And so it was when the new compound fertilisers came out.

Balquhindachy's grieve was an enthusiast for the well-tried husbandry technique of 'huddin on the manure'. And that didn't just mean good honest muck. Whenever he could get the farmer to afford it, he welcomed home loads of guano, which was said to be bat droppings all the way from the caves of South America. Wilson could see it was certainly droppings from some animal, and all the way from somewhere, and there was no doubting that it was growthy stuff. Dried fish heads and bones from the slaughterhouses of Aberdeen gave calcium and some phosphorus, and seaweed from the rocks at Collieston gave iodine, or at least gave something that helped the grass to grow.

So it was with less than the usual scepticism of innovation that Jake Wilson saw the first of the new chemical compound fertilisers arrive home to Balquhindachy. But what he saw when he opened the first bag filled him with scorn. There was no sign of bat's droppings or droppings of any kind, no sign of any bits of bone or seaweed... not even a manurie smell. The new compound manure would clearly be 'nae use ava'.

The grieve wanted to sow this 'fushionless dirt' well away from the road where no-one could see it, or its results. But the farmer would have none of that. Having paid the best part of five pound a ton for the precious stuff (and quite sold on the likely results by the bright-eyed salesman), Baldie was for the new manure being sown on the park that lay open to full view from the New Deer road.

Well, well, the farmer (for all his lack of common sense, which Jake Wilson fine knew wasn't that common) must have his way so they set about sowing the compound fertilisers in the traditional way. The grieve and the first three horsemen donned the happers...the framed canvas or leather basket that rested on

the waist band and hung from shoulder straps.

The precious compound was then loaded into the happers by Willie Anderson, the orraman whose job it would be to keep all four full at all times.

Off they set, four in line and four paces apart, throwing the questionable fertility from them.

I hope I don't give the impression that sowing was in any way a haphazard affair, for it was not. The method was precisely that used in those days to sow cereal crops, and of course those had to be scattered very evenly. That all depended on getting an even pace and a steady throw. You dipped your hand into the happer and drew a handful out and back, then threw out and forward with that hand as the other hand was dipping and drawing back...and all was done in rhythm with the step... each step must have one handful thrown and one hand filled. The man who sows with a happer develops a sort of a swagger as he steps and throws, which has a purpose and a grace which really has to be seen to be appreciated.

At any rate, the four of them made a brave sight from the New Deer road, moving up and down in line, waving their arms in a manner which a stranger might have mistaken for a motion to scare birds, and Willie running between them, making sure they all had something to sow.

All went according to plan, despite the grieve's lack of enthusiasm for the task, until the job was nearly finished. It was an odd-shaped field and so when they had the square finished there was still a wedge of grass which had not received the precious manure. And at that point they ran out. Willie was full of

consternation.

"There's neen left for the gushet, grieve. Fit will we dae?"

If you're a farmer you'll be well able to appreciate Willie's anxiety, for by their failure to make the manure last so as to cover the whole field, they faced public humiliation both long term and short. First, all their neighbours who knew they were trying the new-fangled manure that day would see them leave the gushet unsown and know of their miscalculation. And second, and infinitely worse, if the new chemical fertiliser was any good, every traveller on the road to New Deer would clearly see the evidence all summer. For the grass would surely be a deep green where it had had manure but the gushet would soon be a sickly shade going nearer to grey.

It may be hard for modern folk to understand what the fuss was about. I can hear them say "what would it matter if a wee bit of the field was a different colour from the rest." But it did matter... a great deal, and maybe it still should. It may be all very well for modern workmen, who have their telly to go home to, their weekend run in the car to plan and their holiday in Majorca to worry about, to laugh off a mistake in their work. But when your work was all you had, it was important to get the work right, and when you got it wrong, to try and do it in a park as far from the roadside as possible. But, despite the importance of the problem, and despite the fact that as grieve the blame would stick with him, Jake Wilson was quite unruffled by the prospect and had the perfect answer:

"Awa ye go back and wag yer airms... it'll mak nae difference."

And so it was that the first three horsemen at the great farm of Balquhindachy went back and walked up and down the gushet of the big park that faces the New Deer road, solemnly broadcasting air from empty happers, while Willie the orraman ran up and down with his pails refilling their happers with nothing.

That, of course, got them over the immediate problem of their neighbours knowing that day that they'd got it wrong. But what about the uneven growth of the grass? Well, for all any one of the travellers to and from New Deer noticed, the farmer could have saved his money and manured the whole park the same way as they'd done the gushet.

# CHAPTER TWENTY-NINE

# *Downwardly Mobile*

THE CRAGHALL ESTATE ran to some 12,000 acres in over 100 holdings and yet there can't have been many starker contrasts than that between the neighbouring farms of the Mains and Backhill of Craghall.

As you would expect, the Mains was a big place - 450 acres of the best land on the estate and while it wasn't first class land, it was good. Its gentle, southerly aspect and the fact that it commanded the high ground meant it drained well, grew well, and was always the first place with the binder and first to lead the winter sheaf that signalled the end of harvest.

Now if you went through the close at the Mains with its great byres and barns, and then out over the hill, you'd come to the modest buildings of Backhill of Craghall. That was third class land, and there wasn't even enough of that to make it a good farm. And as well as being north-lying, its bottom two fields were boggy and the top two stony, and to add to that Backhill lay on to the policies of the big house. That meant the tenant of Backhill had to feed the laird's pheasants, his rabbits and his foxes, on top of his other troubles. In fact, when they were discussing what they'd do with the Kaiser after the First World War someone suggested that they make him farm at Backhill of Craghall - and they were only half joking.

Mind you, if you had taken the road through the Mains to Backhill, you'd have noticed another difference. The Mains

127

always had something broken in the close, it was always muddy, and there always seemed to be a beast loose and too many staff not trying hard enough to get it back. The close at Backhill was tidy and busy.

Indeed, in 1930 there was as big a contrast between the two farmers and their wives as there was between the two farms.

Richard Love of the Mains was a delightful chap really. He was as sunny and expansive as Charlie Strachan was dour and careful. Their attitude to horses was typical: Richard Love went to the Great Horse Fair at Aikey and bought the best broken Clydesdales on offer, and, though it was only a four-pair place, the Mains always had five; but Charlie Strachan, who knew his horse flesh, ploughed his farm for nothing. He bought colts, reared and broke them himself, and sold them after one season at a profit.

And Mains, like many of the bigger farmers, always liked to support his smaller neighbours by buying a beast off them at the store sales. He always had to pay a huge price for the one he got from Backhill, and there are those who said that Charlie Strachan got one of his pals to run Richard up deliberately.

Richard Love was too soft with his men and that sapped the morale of the good ones, who left, so that eventually he only had indifferent men whose motto seemed to be: "It'll do if no-one complains." Charlie Strachan didn't need men. He had twenty-four hours every day and he knew only one way to do things - the right way. He did it all himself.

That is, what wasn't done by his equally determined and charmless wife, Jean. She not only did the house and dairy work but at harvest time she stooked, forked to the cart, led the load home, and then built the ricks to Charlie's forking. And dare he lay a sheaf down wrong he heard about it, you can be sure.

That meant Jean was far too busy to do what Penelope did to fill her day. She had her bridge ladies, of course, but she did 'good work' - not least with the Guild. She did the flowers in the church - with flowers from the garden at the Mains, I may say - and she was tireless in visiting the sick and she always had a pot of jam or a few cakes for the old and the poor.

But it was their position in the church that really epitomised the contrast between the two farming teams. Richard Love was a kirk elder, he never missed a Sunday and when the collection was made he put in the only paper money the duty elder ever saw. Charlie Strachan put in something to make a clink when he came to church for Communion twice a year - he was too busy to go more than that.

Their relative status in life was mirrored by their place in church. The Loves sat upstairs in the front row of the gallery, in the seats traditionally reserved for the tenant of the Mains, who, for the last century at least, had always been a Love. The Strachans, on Communion day, had to squeeze in where they could downstairs, but they did notice the way the minister's first look round always included a glance up at the Loves, and just the hint of a bow. It was the same every Sunday.

Well, with that background it should be no surprise that by the depth of the slump in 1933 the Loves' lifestyle in the grand manner, and their lax farming, broke them. A trust deed was signed. But the Strachans meantime had done well, and put a tidy sum in their account at the British Linen Bank in the village.

So that deed moved the Strachans - the only people for miles around with any money - up into the Mains, and the Loves moved over to Backhill.

It was a great day for the Strachans. And with so many people going broke, Charlie was able to buy up poor Richard's machinery and horse for a song. The Strachans had fairly got their reward for all their hard work.

But the poor Loves were devastated. The wee house at Backhill wouldn't take their grand piano, so even it had to go. One doesn't want to dwell too long on their misery, but it has to be explained that what Penelope Love dreaded most was the first day in church. The thought of sitting up there in the gallery in front of everyone in the parish. All eyes upon their suffering - and not all those eyes would be full of sympathy, she could be sure of that.

However, with Richard an elder they couldn't not go, and to feign illness would only set the tongues clacking. And Penelope

Love wasn't a shirker, so on Sunday morning Richard put on his good suit and Penelope put on her beautiful tweed dress with matching coat and hat, and they set off as usual in the Lancia - the new owner hadn't come for that yet.

With thumping hearts they climbed the stairs at five minutes to eleven to face their public humiliation. But if they thought they feared the worst they were wrong. They had not even contemplated the sight that greeted them at the top of the stairs. For there, sitting in the pew the Love family had sat in for over a century, were the Strachans. And they'd brought the new grieve and his

wife as well as their four children, so there wasn't even room in the pew for the Loves, had they been willing to share it.

Poor Richard and Penelope's choice was simple. They could slink off home, or they could go downstairs, withstand the glances, and find themselves a seat among the hoi polloi. Brave people that they were, that was what they did.

## CHAPTER THIRTY

# *Constable Sampson*

THIS IS the story of one of the last of the village bobbies and the mysterious case of why Sandy Sampson never made sergeant.

It certainly wasn't that he wasn't popular because he was. And no wonder for Sandy Sampson was a delightful man, round and rosy and over six feet tall. Indeed he was close to six feet round as well. Once when he was phoning an old friend he hadn't seen for a while, the friend who was hoping he would stop in bye for a blether asked where our man was phoning from:

"Oh I'm phoning from just outside i' phone box at Gleniffer." Aye, it would have been all Sandy could do to get inside a phone box but he had long arms.

And those long arms and the strength of them had made Sandy a champion hammer thrower in his early days - he was too busy being a policeman to be a professional but he was the local champion for years at Gleniffer Games and even went in for the open events where he gave the professionals a good run for their money. There was certainly no doubt in the village that, had he had the training and the time for it, Sandy could have been better than any of them.

Constable Sampson was a real old-fashioned village bobby of the type we could do with bringing back today. He knew everybody in the village and for miles around. If you wanted a spare bit for your tractor he would know who would have one. If anything went missing he'd know where to find it. He didn't clog up the courts with a lot of petty affairs. No one in Gleniffer was ever late with licensing his car for Sandy, who missed nothing, had everybody well warned before their period of grace had run out. The bairns knew better than ride their bikes without lights in winter or come through the halt-stop without stopping for they knew the Bobby would get them...so of course he never had to. And at the Gleniffer dances he'd be there smiling with just that hint of menace that kept everybody in their place.

He really was a public servant. He was there to see that the peace was kept, not to run folks in. After the cattle show or the dances, Sandy would go around taking the car keys off anybody who had had a droppy too much or else he would arrange for a friend who had had a droppy or two fewer to drive them home.

All the farmers in Gleniffer kept their herd-books up to date and even got their agricultural returns in on time because Sandy was always saying he'd be up shortly to see them - though he seldom came.

When I see how little the boys in the squad cars can achieve when they're called out to sort out the youngsters in our village I often think of Sandy. They come up in their car and everybody knows they're coming because they've been well warned by the C.B. network. The car stops for a few minutes or cruises about for a while. They then drive off and all hell breaks out again. But Sandy was always there or thereabouts and he knew which loons needed to be told, which needed their parents to be told, and which needed to feel how strong Sandy's grip could be.

And as well as being a first-rate policeman, Sandy was a real asset to the community. He could, would and indeed had been known to insist on singing and telling stories at parties, and when the football team had needed a new strip it was Sandy who knew someone who would like to make an anonymous donation.

Yes he played his part and, though all was not always as it should have been, any trouble there was almost invariably kept within the village. That was so much so, in fact, that one noted sheriff in Inverness expressed himself amazed to discover that there was a village in Gleniffer at all.

Now Sandy had been a clever youth. He'd got highers at

school and would have gone to university had he not been so set on the police. He'd sat his sergeant's ticket as soon as his two years were out and they say he came top of the exam. Indeed Constable Sampson looked all set to be a high-flyer.

And yet, twenty years later he was still highly thought of, still very well liked and still a constable. Now I wouldn't know if it was true but the man who told me was convinced that Sandy's lack of promotion was all down to what happened on the night of Sandy's second Flower Show dance in Gleniffer.

It had been a lovely do and, in the words of the minister's wife, "everybody had had a droppy but no one had had too much"... not till after the dance that was. But after all had gone quiet, Sandy happened in-bye the Commercial Hotel where he happened to know a few friends were having a quiet one. Now Sandy's day had started before six when he'd been out in his garden lifting his second-prize plate of beetroot for the show so by the small hours of Sunday morning he was ready for a couple of serious hours in the Commercial and felt he'd earned it.

But as bad luck would have it, the Chief Constable had also had a late night. He'd been down at a Masonic dinner in Inverness and was passing through Glenniffer at three in the morning just when Sandy was making his way home too. It was all right for the Chief. He had a driver. But Sandy was walking (or at least he was on foot) a line which was anything but straight, down the middle of the A 147, kicking his policeman's hat in front of him.

The Chief Constable was so unamused that he swore that Constable Sandy Sampson would stay a constable... and so he did for more than twenty years.

## CHAPTER THIRTY-ONE

# *The Ring in the Well*

AGRICULTURAL PROGRESS had really done nothing for Andra. Like a thousand other farmers he'd seen the farm which once employed five men reduced to one man and himself. And while the man got off or got overtime, Andra was never finished. He didn't complain though. He had a no-nonsense matter-of-fact approach which allowed him to see his troubles as challenges rather than tragedies and he got on and did what had to be done without joy but without rancour.

Andra would have seen no reason for Peggy to be anything other than content. She had seen her role through its busiest phase: feeding clothing and chastising the four children and marrying the most likely two off. She was no longer harassed and Peggy would never have doubted that she was happy, though she would never have asked herself such a question. If she had it just might have helped her avoid the trouble they got into the time she lost her wedding ring down the well.

It was one of those ridiculous Pussy-in-the-well things you see in books by Enid Blyton. Peggy had had that built over the old well which had been there since the house was built and had once been its sole source of supply. She'd been tending the flowers she grew in the ornamental wood and brass bucket, when her ring caught on something sharp and fell down the well.

As a good and conventionally brought up girl would be, Peggy was upset. But even she worried at how Andra would feel.

What would he think of the shameless limmer who had let his little band of gold fall in the water?

Well, on that last score at least, she need not have worried one bit.

"I suppose we should be glad your hand s well stucken on," he joked, "or you micht've lost it an aa."

When Peggy started to cry Andra only made things worse with his usual practical approach. "Och, what's in a ring? It only cost two pound ten and mind wi you bein at the College I got ten percent aff. I'll see if I get anither een on Friday so it winna matter if ye lose it again."

When the green pound is overvalued, the cushies are eating the oilseed rape and the overdraft is peeping over its limit, it's hard to remember about being romantic. In fact Andra hardly even noticed. He couldn't hang about. He had beasts to feed and a calf to dose. But even he couldn't forget the incident altogether. Peggy saw to that. She pestered and pestered at him to get that ring out of the well.

She became more and more irritable as women do, and, as husbands often do, he took as little notice as possible. It was all sorts of silly little things. Peggy never ate anything between meals but now, when Andra was having a polo mint to ease his indigestion, it was,"And am I nae gettin a sweetie."

"Oh, sorry love. Wid ye like een?"

"No thank, you," she would say frostily.

There was a lot of that sort of thing. The complaints at him: drying his greasy hands on the dish towels; bringing straw in and scattering it all over the house; not taking his wellingtons off when he was just in to make a quick phone call and it was hardly worth it for all the mess you could make in a few minutes. Peggy complained about all those perfectly reasonable things that Andra had been doing all the years of their marriage.

What made things worse for Peggy was that Andra would never do anything about her complaints. Nor would he fight back at all. He just said "Oh aye", canny like and carried on regardless.

I suspect that anyone who has been married for a few years and can't recognise the scene is either a saint, married to one, or

135

a liar.

Soon everything was annoying Peggy so that even Andra's even keel started to rock. He was driven to try a reasoned appeal but that was worse than a failure. "Ye promised to tak me for better or waur," he said.

"Well, it's waur!" was all the encouragement he got.

To cut a long and discouraging story short, the day came when even Andra could see that the well would have to be drained.

It wasn't an easy job. It looked like it was only maybe eight feet to the bottom and that was soon pumped out. But it was a very old well and had been disused since the big grants for new wells came in after the war. That meant that for forty years no one cared what the children threw down the old well to hear the splash, never mind what had fallen into it in the two hundred years before that.

So when the water was out and it was down to the mud, and Andra had lowered his ladder in to start the search for the ring, the ladder just kept on going and was soon out of sight. Before he could get a firm base to start his excavations, Andra had to go for the extending ladder.

Day after day, one bucket load at a time, the well gave up its secrets. Every load had to be sifted in case the ring be overlooked.

It was a sore usurper of Andra's time but, after a while, he began to enjoy it as a challenge. He was fascinated by the trock that turned up. The well was like an archeologist's trench. It gave little clues to the family history at every bucketful. Like the roller skate he used to have and of which his little brother Sandy had been so jealous. He had thought the little brat had taken it but never thought of the well. He found a rickle of sticks which was just recognisable as one of the jumping monkeys the bothy lads used to make. There was the awl he could clearly remember his granny using to darn his father's socks and the last on which Andra's father had done all the minor repairs to their boots when he'd been a boy.

Peggy's humour improved greatly during the excavation of the well. What a good man Andra was really. Doing all that

136

digging just for her. He maybe wasn't very good at showing it normally, but when he had so much to do on the farm it fairly showed that he did love her really.

Andra had told her that you can't raise water more than twenty eight feet so when they were down to twenty-five feet Peggy knew it wouldn't be long. And when Andra came in all smiles that day she was filled with affection for the big soft lump she had married.

"Look what I've found next," he crowed. "Dae ye ken what this is? It's the auld throwin hammer the boys from the bothy used to throw of a summer's evenin. Dad threw at the games and got a third eence at Gight in the open. It's jist what we need for swipin the lums. Far better than yer new-fangled brushes and suction. Ye see, ye tie yer rope to the head by threadin it through the hole then ye lower it doon the lum. Ony starries' nests or knots o' soot dinna stand a chance. Feel the weight o' that."

Peggy had no desire to feel the weight of anything. "And what about my wedding ring," she said.

"Oh aye. We got it an aa. Ye'll find it.... oh aye it's on the breeze block at the ither side o' the waal. Ye see, being gold it had sunk through time richt tae the bottom o the waal... jist like the hammer heid."

# CHAPTER THIRTY-TWO

# *Fifteen Poun for a Neep*

IT HAPPENED one day when Gibby Gordon was doing his rounds of the cattle he was fattening. He liked to be out early and it was just as well, for he had stots scattered all over the country. He didn't like to pay too much when he was taking grass so he went to all the grass roups in the spring and just took a parkie here and a parkie there when it was cheap.

Anyway, this morning he was well off on his rounds when he had a puncture. Some bad language (which nobody heard) and he was into the boot only to discover that the spare wheel was flat as well. There was a fine kettle of fish. He could hardly go to anybody's house and use their phone as it was not yet six o'clock. Still he didn't want to be behind all day over one puncture. So Gibby Gordon decided to do what he did not do often - he would walk.

It was a beautiful morning. The sun was shining with that dazzle you usually only get from snowy sunshine, but which you sometimes see in an early summer's morning before the dew has been steamed off the grass to make haze. The dawn chorus was just past its peak but still welcoming the new day, and Gibby rather enjoyed the raucous peacefulness which was usually denied him by his Range-Rover.

The whole thing reminded the farmer of when he was a boy

and went with six other loonies and quinies along the road each morning - walking the three and a half miles to Whitestripes school. He remembered the rows they used to get for being late, casting about in the newly breered parks for peesie's nests in the springtime. How they used to guddle for the trouts they could see from the brig over Lonie's burn. And he remembered how in autumn they would stop at a park full of turnips, jump in over the dyke, grab a neep, break it on the top of the dyke and eat the crisp juicy flesh. A fresh neep had been just as sweet as any apple and a lot easier to come by in those days.

Gibby chuckled as he remembered the time he'd been jumping in-over a neep park and had caught his breeks on the barbed-wire and torn them. And he shuddered when he remembered the hiding he'd got when he'd gone home - for tearing his breeks you understand, not for stealing. No one would have grudged a bairn a neep.

It suddenly occurred to him that this was that very same park, though it had been re-fenced by then. And lo and behold it was in neeps again. They were well shawed and real tempting.

Now Gibby Gordon was not a man given to impetuous or childlike behaviour but he was overcome by the atmosphere and the nostalgia and without more than a moment's thought he was in-over the dyke and selecting a nice small juicy neep. He pulled it up, shook off the worst of the earth and smashed it over a stone on top of the dyke. He then trimmed the shaws and was all set with what used to pass, with the children of Whitestripes, for an iced-lolly thirty years earlier.

Gibby was savouring his second mouthful when his mood of quiet reverie was rudely shattered;

"What the hell do you think you're doing?" shouted a voice that originated south of the Wash and had clearly learned how to deal with strangers on the playing fields of Eton or some such.

"Oh, good morning," said Gibby, "I'm jist haein a neep. They're right sweet. Grand mornin, isn't it?"

"And do you realise whose turnip it is?" roared the voice which was becoming apoplectic.

Well, by this time Gibby has figured that out all right. The

man was obviously a foreigner - townser probably - made his
money out of property or the law or something and had no
understanding of the ways of the countryside.

"Oh, look here. I'm sorry about this but you see when I was
a bairn..."

"Sorry, is it? Is that all you can say when I catch you stealing
my turnips? You're a thief and a vandal scrambling over my
stone wall."

Gibby was a patient man but by this time he had had enough:

"Here's a pound for your neep and if that's nae enough for
you, put a cart up to Greenies and I'll gie ye a whole load."

Gibby stalked off quivering with rage. The beautiful morning had fairly been spoiled.

But he hadn't seen anything yet. By ten o'clock the police
were up at Greenies;

"Gilbert Gordon?"

"Ye ken fine it's me Sergeant. Fit is't?" said Gibby
his temper still shortened by the events of the morning but
never dreaming there was any connection between those
and the policeman's visit.

"You are charged that at or about six am on Thursday
the twenty-fifth of September, 1982, you did take a neep
unlawfully out of the roadside park at Hillside of

Whitestripes, the property of Geoffrey Tennent-Smythe," Sergeant Mathieson read out laboriously.

Gibby was flabbergasted. "But I offered him the price of a hale bag of neeps and telt him to come up for a cairt load ony time he liked," he protested.

It was no use. There was no way back and Gibby landed in court. He told the judge he was surprised that the court was interested but that he was guilty... that he had indeed taken that neep.

But that wasn't the end of the matter for Gibby lost his cool altogether when he heard the court's decision:

"Fifteen poun for a neep?" he roared. "That's nae justice. I'm nae payin fifteen poun for a neep. I'd rather go to jail."

And that's how the farmer of the Greens of Whitestripes landed in Peterhead prison for eating a neighbour's neep when he had thirty acres of his own to choose from. Gibby reflected sadly to himself that at fifteen pounds a neep his thirty acres must be worth about five million pounds... and that anybody entering the market at that sort of price would soon fill his shed.

The cell door slammed shut; it was hardly the way Gibby had been expecting to spend that Friday. He would fairly be the speak o' the mart.

As Gibby's eyes gradually got used to the gloom he became aware that he was not alone in the cell. The shape of an old man appeared. He was ragged and dirty with long silver hair that straggled over a face that was deathly white. "The Count of Monte Cristo," Gibby thought to himself, but it was just an ordinary long-term prisoner.

"What are ye in for son" said the shape.

"Oh I took a neep fae a neighbour's park and got fourteen days for it rather than pay the fine." said Gibby. "What about yoursel?"

"I'm in my twenty-third year of a life sentence for rape," said the old man.

"Good god!" said Gibby. "You must have been affa hungry... did ye eat a hale park?"

# CHAPTER THIRTY-THREE

# *Mulligatawny*

HIS NAME was Tony Mulligan, though nobody called him that. He'd been in the Inniskilling Volunteers in the First War, you see, and it was there that he got the nickname by which he was known affectionately all his later days. They'd been having a roll call, and the sergeant was bawling out the names:

"Flannagan, James."

"Aye Sir."

"MacAskill, David."

"Aye Sir."

"Mulligan, Tony."

But Tony's mind had wandered to the park of stots across the road.

"Mulligan Tony," roared the sergeant, who knew fine Tony was there, "If you don't answer you'll be right in the soup." And from that day onwards, he was always known as Mulligatawny.

And that wasn't the only important decision taken that day, for while he was looking at those steers grazing, Mulligatawny made up his mind that if he got back alive from France, he would become a cattle dealer. By the grace of God he did get back from France, which is more than his three brothers did, and with his parents gone, that meant that Mulligatawny could sell the croft and buy his first twenty calves to sell to the rich farmers of Scotland.

That was a big trade in those days, especially from the west of Ireland where all the crofters, and there were millions of them, had a cow for milk, but where nearly everyone was too poor to eat beef. That meant the calves were "easy for to buy", as Mulligatawny said, and they were easy to sell in Scotland, where the rich grazers in the Lothians, Fife and the North-east had the markets of London, never mind Edinburgh, to supply.

So Mulligatawny sold his twenty calves to advantage, and went back for another thirty. Before long, he was bringing steers over by the hundred. Now, on the whole, dealers aren't very popular - farmers tend to look down on them as parasites though it is admitted, if grudgingly, that they do have their uses sometimes. But even the most grudging of farmers had to like Mulligatawny. He was honest for a start, he had good cattle, and he was always so cheery.

"If you don't bid up lads, old Mulligatawny'll be in the soup again," he would say and though everyone had heard it before and no one thought it very funny the first time, they still had to laugh. Many a poor widow got a bargain from Mulligatawny. He never pushed hard for his money, and he had such charm that he could make a half crown luck penny feel like a fiver:

"Ah yes sir, you made a right shrewd purchase there." he would say.

So everyone was genuinely startled and saddened when Mulligatawny went broke. Mind you, the clacking tongues said it was no wonder, he was always too cheap. There may have been something in that, but I think it was his market philosophy which did for him. If he took his stock to market and couldn't sell them, he reckoned the market must be cheap and started to buy. Well, that worked out not too badly until the catastrophic slide in store cattle prices in 1933. Mulligatawny had started buying in the spring, and by autumn he had cattle stashed all over Scotland, eating him out of house and home. Eventually, in agreement with the major creditors, the mart, he broke. His debts came to over £19,000 and the marts started to sell the cattle off to square the accounts.

However, the sales went well and the market started to pick up on the run up to Christmas. Because he was so popular, there were always people there to make sure nobody stole Mulligatawny's cattle. The great day eventually came when the debts were down to £1157 and the cattle were down to one cross-Highland cow with a second-cross Shorthorn calf at foot. It was a good enough calf, but the total value of the outfit couldn't possibly have exceeded £20 or so. Every farmer for miles around crowded into the market at Aberdeen for Mulligatawny's last sale. And he was cheery as ever, though you could see he was having to try awful hard. He went through his usual routine. The bidding got up to £18 and Mulligatawny, shaking his head, said:

"No no, boys, I'll need more for this one. Look at that calf, he'll be a grower yet, that one." But the bidding stuck fast at £22. He said it for the last time as a sort of farewell speech, and a thankyou for the good times:"Aye, Mulligatawny's in the soup this time." The smile was warm, but you couldn't help noticing the tear.

Then a strange thing happened. The cow and calf had been bought by one of the stingiest farmers in Aberdeenshire, a man who had once sacked a good cattleman for stealing the thirds off the thrashing mill to feed to his hens.

"Put her up again," he said.

So the auctioneer started again. Now that farmer's name was Reid, and he had a neighbour called McIntosh. They were good neighbours, but jealous. McIntosh had always said, though privately, that Reid would take the last penny off a tink wife, he was so mean. At any rate, having given back the cow and calf, it is said that Reid turned deliberately and glowered at McIntosh.

Well, that did it. McIntosh couldn't possibly pay less than that skinflint Reid, so he made sure that he bought the cow and calf for £23.

"Put her up again," he said.

Now Willie Pidduck, the dealer, could see how things were going. He liked Mulligatawny, and he dealt in dairy cattle anyway, so he wasn't a competitor. And he would show his generosity, and that his business was on a sound footing:

"Twenty-five pounds," he roared out.

Then all the other dealers had to take their turn at buying the cow, and soon the farmers and the dealers were competing to show that they too were fit to buy the cow and calf. In the space of ten minutes, the cow was put up and returned 47 times, and Mulligatawny had avoided bankruptcy.

He stood bewildered in the ring, tears streaming down his cheeks, until one of the auctioneers whispered something in his ear. He straightened, went out through one of the small gates, shook hands with his saviours, many of whom had done the only good turn they had ever done. Then sadly he made for the old Albion lorry which had dragged so many cattle across Ireland and across Scotland. It would take him home, and he'd rest a while with his sisters. It had been a tiring time, even for a man of his optimism.

He hadn't gone far down the road when he thought he felt a movement from the back of the lorry. He got out to check his tyres, to be greeted by a bellow from the float, and there was the cow and the calf.

Mulligatawny was born again. He dealt on successfully for another twenty years, still cheerful, but a lot more careful.

# CHAPTER THIRTY-FOUR

# *The Meeting*

THERE HAS arisen in the countryside, in recent years, a rash of those bogus parties where farmers are invited to have a drink, and maybe even a bite to eat, while some tame expert extols the virtues of certain products - and the additional advantages of buying them from their hosts. These are a sort of farmers' Tupperware party and foremost in their promotion have been the drug companies... just about the only people who've made any money out of agriculture in recent years. Well this is the story of a young drug salesman and the hard time he had in the winter of 1986 running one such evening.

The party was to be held in the Commercial Hotel in a wee village that stands on the edge of one of those areas where nature has been rather meagre with her bounty, where heather and bracken are easier to grow than wheat or potatoes but where a hardy band of small farmers cling to the hillsides using the time-worn formula of livestock and endless toil.

It was a damnable night of snow and just enough wind to put the fear of drifting into anyone thinking of going out for the evening, so Alisdair Duguid wasn't expecting a big audience and that expectation proved prophetic, for at 7.30 pm only one man had turned up.

As you can imagine, Alisdair was embarrassed. He smiled nervously at the waitresses and blushed when he recalled insisting to the manageress that she would need to lay on a hundred and twenty plates of stovies just in case. The audience, as it happened, was a thick-set man but there was no way he was going to make much impression on a hundred and twenty platefuls of stovies.

Alisdair offered his lonely victim a drink "while we wait and see if there's anybody else." It wasn't a brilliant conversation but it did emerge that 'Mr MacDonald' farmed eight miles away up a Glen at a place the salesman couldn't quite catch.

At a quarter to eight Alisdair decided to call the whole thing off. The stovies would keep and it was hardly worth it for an audience of one anyway;

"And wouldn't you be better to get away up the road Mr Macdonald, before the roads block?"

But Mr MacDonald hadn't come all that way to hear about the 'Prevention and Cure of Liverfluke' to be put off that easily.

"Na, na laddie, that winna dae. If I gang tae a' the bother to fill a cairt o' neeps, drive it up the hill to feed my ewes and only find one, I dinna leave her to starve." Mr MacDonald rose from the bar, marched over to where the chairs were set out, sat down in the eighth row, folded his considerable arms and stared fixedly at the platform.

Considerably chastened, Alisdair Duguid made his presentation, determined to make a job of it. Nothing was left out. He made his address of welcome with the joke in it. There was the vote of thanks to the staff for the excellent stovies which they would be serving in due course. Then the talk on the liverfluke with the slides on the overhead projector. And of course there was the audio-visual on how the drug company's products would end the problem for a very reasonable investment; 'Liver-right' would cure the disease while 'Snail-it' would ensure that it never recurred by clearing the snails that spread the disease.

Then it was "Any questions?"

But Mr MacDonald, whose arms were still folded, and who hadn't stirred nor taken his eyes off the platform, didn't have any questions.

Remembering about the feeding of the ewes the young salesman proceeded to answer the questions he knew from

147

experience the audience would have asked had more of them turned up - it gave him another chance to extol the virtues of Snail-it and Liver-right anyway.

It was about ten o'clock when Alisdair Duguid finished.

"How was that Mr MacDonald?" he said.

Mr MacDonald moved for the first time in two and a quarter hours;

"Ower lang," he said, emphasising just how much can be conveyed with just two words.

The salesman was quite taken aback

"But Mr MacDonald, you said yourself that if you'd carted a load of turnips up the hill to feed your ewes and only one turned up, you didn't leave her to starve."

"Aye, aye," said the farmer, "but if I've only the ae ewe I dinna gie her the hale load."

## CHAPTER THIRTY-FIVE

# Way Tae Me

IT WAS in 1979 and the British were trying to establish a sheep industry to help the poor Colombian peasants who were trying to scrape a cold living off the bare hillsides at between 10,000 and 16,500 feet. They had imported Scottish Blackfaces to cross with the local Creolla sheep to produce a hardy greyfaced ewe to put back to the local tups.

I heard about it from Ian Skea, an Orkney man I met at Aberdeen University and later stumbled across in Kenya where he was breeding goats, one of the many farming jobs he has done throughout the world for various development agencies. The Blackies to the Andes was another of Skeas projects.

Incidentally, it worked very well, but Skea and his team had terrible bother with the Blackies which they had to breed pure to maintain the supply of tups. The problem was failure to breed and the reason, they eventually decided, was that they were at the equator where summer and winter are much like spring and autumn, and the Scottish Blackface ewe relies on the approach of the icy blast of winter to let her know that it's time to come in heat.

But that was neither the biggest nor the first snag to hit the new Technical Co-operation Officer. That was, undoubtedly, the fact that everyone on the project, as in the rest of Colombia, would speak Spanish. Now Ian's employers could see all that and so they had sent him to London for a crash course in the language.

But London was a big change from Orkney or even Aberdeen, and the enquiring mind would take our man to all the sights of London. By day, he and his Shetlander wife Rosemary investigated the Tower of London, Madam Tussauds, Kew Gardens and in the evenings, the bright lights of the West End. A great time was had by both, but in the end the only thing that crashed was the course.

It wasn't too bad at the airport in Bogata because there, there was always somebody who could speak some English, and anyway he was met by the embassy staff - but it was then that it first dawned on the new TCO that a little attention to the studies might well have been a good idea, for everyone was speaking Spanish and even the gents was called something different, if there was one.

The feeling of unease grew into something like panic as he approached the sheep station. How could you put men to their work if you couldn't speak the language?

It was a cold and misty day at 10,000 feet in the Andes. He could have been at home on a steep in Orkney if it hadn't been for the fact that he was sat on a mule and that his backside was extremely uncomfortable after two hours there.

And then, faintly at first and then quite distinctly, out of the mist came music to our man's ears. It was the unmistakable sound of a Scottish sheepdog being worked. "Way tae me, Spot. Way tae me, way tae me. Canny noo, canny noo Spot, come bye, come bye, that'll do Spot. Lie doon."

"Well, at least there's somebody here that can speak the language, and if there's one maybe there's plenty. And even if he is the only man that can speak English I can use him to interpret to the rest." Skea nudged his mule towards where the noise had come from. Eventually, out of the mist a figure started to appear. It was soon obvious that it was not to be a Scottish shepherd, somehow transported seven thousand miles to the left and down a bit. It was, in fact, a large figure under a wide sombrero and inside a poncho, smoking a Clint Eastwood slim cigar.

"Buenas Dias Senor. Com esta," he said.

"Aye, aye, how are you. I'm the new TCO from Scotland.

I'm quite relieved to hear you can speak English. Where did you learn to speak like that?"

"Que?" came the baffled reply. It was not the reply for which Ian Skea was hoping. And it soon became clear that the only words of English that Senor Jose Garcia could speak were the ones with which he had been commanding his working dogs.

So how had that come about? Well, as part of the project to develop sheep in the high Andes, MacDonald Frasers, the Perth Auctioneers, had sent out a load of Scottish collies. They were already trained, of course, and it was thought impractical to retrain them with Spanish commands, so they taught the Colombian shepherds to use the Scottish commands.

Of course, as is always the case when you are thrown into a situation like that, Senor Skea was soon talking Spanish, if not like a Spaniard or a Colombian, at least as well as a Scot who has been to a crash course in London. And the shepherds are still talking Scots to their dogs, even though most of those that are working there were bred in Colombia off the original imports, and though they hear everyone else around them getting their orders (and their characters) in Spanish.

## CHAPTER THIRTY-SIX

# *Tell a Good Lie*

THIS IS a true story about that sweetest but most exhausting of times - the lambing. The villain is my great grandfather, John Mackie.

It had been a hectic lambing at Milton of Noth in Rhynie. The three hundred ewes had seemed all to want to lamb at night. They were none too strong either for it had been a bad year for hay with a long course winter.. and, mind you, April the first is still winter on the north slopes of the Tap o' Noth.

But Alex Thomson the shepherd had done a wonderful job. For four weeks he had dedicated himself to the lambs, snatching only the odd wink of sleep between crises.

So when John Mackie arrived in his gig to see his outfarm, the shepherd was just about done in. For all that, good man that he was, he was hurrying home to grab a bite of supper before another night's vigil.

My great grandfather summed up the situation immediately. He ordered his man home to his supper and assured him that the farmer would take care of the night shift. He didn't want to see his man until he'd had a good night's sleep.

John Mackie had three farms at the time. There was the home farm at Auchnagatt, the one at Tarves ten miles away and the hill farm at Rhynie, a short day's drive away by gig. There he had a housekeeper who kept everything right for him and fed him when he came on his rounds. At Tarves the strapper and his wife kept

the farmhouse, reserving a room for their boss's convenience.

Now my great grandfather, whom I never met, was a most attractive man. He was good looking in the manner of the time, witty, interested and interesting. He had what is now known as 'charisma'.

So when John Mackie arrived at one of his outfarms, the word soon got round and his friends would gather to share his company, his whisky and his billiard table of which he had three, one in each of his farmhouses.

And so it was that April evening when John Mackie visited his outfarm at Rhynie. After supper he checked the ewes and their lambs. Certainly the shepherd had done a wonderful job against all the odds.

He went through the byres. The cattle were looking well and everything was tidy. There were plenty of neeps in and corn, and there was enough left in the cornyard for two days' thrashing - one for the beasts and one to sell.

Yes, John Mackie was well pleased with how things were going on his hill farm when the first of his friends arrived.

The housekeeper had laid in plenty of whisky and cheese. She had done a special baking of oatcakes and made a dumpling. With five of his best pals, the flower of Rhynie's middle-aged, John Mackie was all set for a great night of conversation and billiards.

The old man was reckoned a brilliant conversationalist but, by all accounts he was an absolute wizard at billiards. I can believe it for he taught his son, my grandfather, to play and he, in his eighties could still play a shot which I found quite remarkable. Using top spin, not all that side and bottom they use in snooker nowadays, but topspin, he could put both balls in the same pocket even if they were nowhere near in line.

On this night the conversation and the billiards and food and drink at the roaring fire proved of more immediate interest to my great grandfather than his sheep - or his promise to the shepherd.

Suddenly it was five o'clock in the morning and he remembered; "Oh my god! The ewes!"

John Mackie and his remaining two guests rushed out to see the sheep. Luckily only one had lambed. It had one fine strong lamb happily sucking and one, newly born, dead.

What a disaster! Not the loss of a lambie, you understand, but the loss of face at not having kept his side of the bargain. There was no doubt that the shepherd, exhausted as he was, would much rather have watched his sheep than slept had he suspected such neglect.

There was nothing else for it. The lamb would have to be buried and the shepherd would never be any the wiser.

But where to bury it? The obvious place was the midden which was fine and soft, and an easy place to dig.

When my great grandfather met the shepherd the next morning he said," Oh aye, shepherd, I lookit the ewes last nicht. There was just one, a single."

"A single was it?" roared the shepherd. "Then what the hell was that I got this mornin, rinnin aboot the midden and baain for its mither?"

The warmth of the muck had been all the lambie had needed for life, and the old man's laziness had meant that he had only to win clear of some loose straw.

There should really be a moral to that story but there isn't. I have an old friend who gave me one that would do. He used to say, "If you're gaun to tell a lie, tell a good een."

154

# CHAPTER THIRTY-SEVEN

# The Lumberjack

ALL MY stories have some truth in them. Some have more truth than others but I can't say that this is one of those. I came across Jimmy when I went to work in Glasgow in 1962. It was quite an experience going from rural Aberdeenshire to living in the real Glasgow - up a close in a tenement.

In Aberdeenshire we never had smog. In Glasgow we had to wash the net curtains every two weeks if we wanted to see through them. On the worst day, you could see the other end of the living room but not that clearly - mind you, it was a big living room and it was thirty-five years ago. I was in what I think was the last of the pea soup fogs. I had to sit down for a rest while on the way to the dentist's because with the air being so full of fog there wasn't enough room for oxygen.

As an east-coaster going west I had read up about Glasgow. I had learned of the Irish connection and that led me to expect a lot of Billies and Tims. But what shocked me for a start was that there appeared to be so many Jimmies. My first close contact with Glaswegians en masse was when they were taking down the tenement next door. They arrived each morning like the dawn chorus in a rookery;

"Hallo rerr, Jimmy, aw right?"

"Aye fine Jim. How's yer farra?"

"Watch who yer shovin Jimmy."

"C'mon Jimmy, get aff."

It took me a while to grasp that Jimmy was the Glaswegian equivalent to pal, buddy, or my good fellow in other parts of the world.

But my hero really was called Jimmy. His father who was also called Jimmy, worked in the Fairfield shipyard in Govan, went to Ibrox for the big games, and drank George Younger's light ale in what passed at that time in Govan for moderation. He was a fitter, proud of his trade and proud of his class.

Auld Jimmy had tried to get Jimmy to follow him as a fitter or even try for another trade in the yard, but the lad was one of those who would be different. He was good with his hands and easily clever enough to have got an apprenticeship with his family connections. That was really what his father wanted because though Jimmy was wiry he was awful wee and was certainly not built for labouring.

But Jimmy would leave school and Govan at fifteen. No one really knew where he went. There was mention of Africa and doing well but here he was back in Govan, out of work, out of touch and broke.

There could be no question of a trade now. In those days, if you didn't get an apprenticeship when you were sixteen, that was that.

Eventually his father, embarrassed by having a son with no trade and on the dole, showed Jimmy an advert in the Evening News. It was for a lumberjack in Canada. "Aw right," said Jimmy, "I'll try for it."

To cut a very long story short, Jimmy eventually arrived at the lumberjacking camp in Macpherson's Creek set halfway up the canyon among the redwoods, some of which were said to be three hundred feet high and a thousand years old. He knocked at the door of the log cabin.

The ganger, Big Red, a lumbering giant of a man, looked clear over Jimmy's head when he answered the door. "Funny," he said, "I could have swore there was a knockin at the door."

"Doon here, ye big ape," said Jimmy, his long training in the Glasgow School of Charm shining through.

The lumberjack looked down, "Oh hallo, Sonny," he said

kindly, "What can ah do for yah?"

"A'm after the job in the paper," said Jimmy, "And never mind the 'Sonny', by the way."

"You a lumberjack?... Ho ho, ha ha, he he," said Big Red, much less kindly. "No, no. We need real men for this lumberjackin business. Sorry Sonny, but you're just too small."

"Gonny gie's a trial? Ah've came a lang road for this job. It's the least ye's can dae. And, Jimmy, gonny stop callin me Sonny?" said Jimmy.

"OK son, I'll give ye a trial. Take this here hatchet and cut us some kindling sticks from that pile of redwoods over there."

"Ok. Nae borra. Geis a haud o yer ex and would you mind no callin me 'Son' all the time, by the way."

The lumberjack went off inside chuckling at the cheek of the wee Scotsman. "No more'n knee high to a grasshopper and thinks he'd manage lumberjackin." He got the can on for a new brew of coffee. Jimmy went off to the pile of redwoods to hack sticks.

Big Red was pouring himself his first mug of coffee from the new brew when another knock came at the door of the log cabin. Big Red always liked the first of the new brew. It had so much better a flavour than the acrid tar that remained after a brew had been hottering on the stove for hours. "Goldarnit," he said, "who the hell next?"

It was wee Jimmy from Glasgow. "Zat aw right?" he said pointing to where the redwood logs had been. Big Red had difficulty in believing his eyes for there, where there had been a lorry load of redwood logs, stood the biggest pile of kindling he had ever seen - and neatly stacked at that.

Wee Jimmy could see that Red was impressed, "Have ah got the job then?"

"Well now Sonny,... ah... that is some impressive but Ah don't know. Our lumberjacks are usually a mite bigger'n you. Do you think you could handle a full man-sized axe?"

"What are ye wantin done wi it," asked Jimmy, eager enough to overlook being called 'Sonny' for once.

"You see them thar redwoods up at the top of the canyon thar? Well, you go up thar an cut yourself a couple, brash-em, split-em and stack-em ready for transportation."

"Aw right, Big Yin," said Jimmy, "Gie's yer ex." And away he went whistling up the canyon with the great axe over his shoulder.

Big Red was just pouring himself his second cup of coffee, and reflecting on how the second was never as flavoursome as the first cup, when another knock came to the cabin door. "Huh! That'll be that damned Scotchman come to admit defeat. Poor kid. I suppose I'll need to refund his bus fare."

It was Wee Jimmy from Govan, right enough. "Zat aw right then, Jimmy," he said gesturing with his thumb over his shoulder up the canyon to where the redwoods had been.

Big Red couldn't believe his eyes. The entire south side of the valley had been cleared of trees and every fifty yards or so was a neat stack of timber, all brashed and split and ready for transportation.

Big Red was impressed. "Well Son, I guess you get the job. But tell me, where the hell did you learn your loggin?"

"The Sahara Desert," said Jimmy, "and cut oot cryin me Son, will ye?"

Now, Big Red might have misjudged this Glaswegian but he wasn't as thick as he looked and he knew a bit of geography. "Come off it Scotchman, you cain't fool me. There ain't no trees in the Sahara Desert."

"Granted," said Wee Jimmy, "No noo."

## CHAPTER THIRTY-EIGHT

# *The Millionaires*

MRS HAMILTON had been looking forward to George's retirement for years really. Twenty-five years in the bank house had been more than enough. It had been all right living in the grand Victorian mansion when the children had been young. But they had left years ago and the banker and his wife had ached to get away to the cosy little rose-gardened cottage they'd bought for their retirement.

A smart move that had been - buying the cottage. A low-interest loan from the bank, inflation and a good tenant who'd not only paid the loan back but lavished as much love on the garden as George Hamilton would do in his retirement, had made it an excellent speculation.

In fact the Hamiltons were going to retire - not to put it too vulgarly - rich. George had always been careful with money. He'd saved a little, even in those early days as a teller and he'd invested the money wisely. He'd put half into insurances and half into ordinary shares. The insurances had all matured on his retirement but it was the stock exchange which had really paid off for the Hamiltons - for George had hit on a plan that worked, and stuck to it. Whatever advice the bank's market analysts were giving, he would do the opposite. It didn't always work but when it did it paid handsomely as George Hamilton was one of the few who had guessed right on those occasions.

And then there was the bank pension, and for that they decided to take a lump sum. Oh yes, the Hamiltons in their retirement would be distinctly 'well-to-do'.

And that's important when you've been a banker all your working days and bowed the rich in and out of your office daily, and daily refused to lend money to anyone who had real need of it.

Well, well, retirement day had come and gone. The bank had made Mr Hamilton a beautiful presentation - a silver salver and ever so heavy. And the Hamiltons had decided to start retirement in the grand manner - with a Mediterranean cruise. They would see St Mark's Square in Venice, the Parthenon, the Acropolis and the Holy Land - all of which they could well afford.

And so it was that the strangest friendships got up. For, on that cruise and travelling first class at that was, as he himself put it, a small farmer from the Howe of Strathmore in Angus. Bob Clark and his wife Gladys were from a far tougher mould than the Hamiltons. He'd started with a puckly hens in one of his father's back fields and built up from there. Though he'd long since stopped grafting on the farm he had, and always would have, working hands.

But in the odd way that friendships can work, the retired banker and the retiring farmer hit it off. The banker was able to explain to the farmer why it was that banks who make money by lending money were always so loath to lend any. And the farmer patiently explained why potato harvesting was so often left to the wet days of October instead of being done in the sunny days of June.

But the two couples' real bond was formed through bridge. They were, all four of them, addicts and of a similar high standard. The fact that the farmer tended to over-bid his hand while the banker under-bid his, lent a piquancy to the battles which were only punctuated briefly by meals and occasionally by the need for sleep.

For all the Hamiltons and the Clarks saw of St Mark's Square and the Parthenon and the Acropolis, they might just as well have stayed at home. Mind you, Mrs Hamilton did draw the line at a quick hand instead of the two-hour tour of Jerusalem - after all, her bridge ladies would need a report on that.

And it was Mrs Hamilton who noticed something about the Clarks. When Mr Clark was brought change he would take it all or leave the coppers - unlike the banker who would wave his well-to-do hand expansively and say "keep the change". And Mr Clark had been a bit slow to say yes to that Chateaubriand steak they'd decided to share, and which cost extra. So Mrs Hamilton decided her friends - for all they were travelling first class - were in fact not very well off, just putting on a brave face. She persuaded her husband to pick up the bills wherever they went and whence-so-ever they came. And so he did. And there were no signs from the Clarks of resentment or embarrassment. "Friendship is worth that," thought Mrs Hamilton, "and after all, we can afford it."

And Mrs Hamilton took quite a shine to Mr Clark. The rough farmer was so good at bridge, had a sense of humour of his own, and with just a bit more education and a bit more drawing out - well who could know? She did her best:

"We're passing Venice now Mr Clark, that's where the Pope stays. They've stopped to see the Parthenon, Mr Clark, that's stood for a thousand years." And "Oh, the Acropolis Mr Clark,

161

that's where the Romans fed Christians to the lions".

"Oh aye," was about as much as she got for a reply.

But one day she came bustling up a minute or two late for the after-dinner session. The bridge players were - as bridge players are always - unamused.

"I'm sorry I'm late but I was speaking to the other ladies," she said in some excitement, "and Mr Clark, do you know there are four millionaires on this ship?"

Mr Clark looked startled,

"Do you tell me that, Mistress Hamilton? And there was me thinking there was five of us."

# CHAPTER THIRTY-NINE

# *The Rivals*

WILLIE AND Alexander had been bairns together and they'd always been rivals. It was really no more than you'd expect, for both stood out among their contemporaries and, throughout their lives, as little cubs, as young bucks, even as old bulls they always tried to best one another.

At first it was just the childish competitions at school; who would be "it", whose turn was it next, and, interminably, who had won. And if their disputes ended in a fight you could be sure both would be crying before it finished for they were both as determined as they were competitive.

As the two progressed through life the games changed, of course but the competition remained just as fierce. If William fancied a girl then Alexander would fancy her too - and if Alexander couldn't win her away from his rival he would aver loudly that she was a right tink but maybe good enough for Willie.

Like all the young men before the Great War, they used to throw the hammer and the fifty-sixer and put the shot in the Summer evenings which in those days were longer and sunnier. Willie was the best hammer thrower but wasn't so far ahead that Alexander wouldn't compete. And on the one evening that Alexander did win they say that Willie threw and threw until it was dark, trying to assert his ascendancy, but on that occasion he failed.

The rivalry was natural really for Willie and Alexander were the eldest sons from two farms which glowered across the river Don at one another, and as you can imagine the rivalry only intensified when each succeeded to his father's tenancy.

Alexander's was a good bit the bigger place and could boast three pairs of horse. Willie had only a two-pair place but he had the south face of the valley, so he could always sow and reap that day earlier, and in a difficult harvest Alexander would have to watch in fury as Willie got that hour's advantage as they dodged the sheaves home between showers.

Alexander's extra acres fairly gave him the edge though. He was the first to have a reaper binder and he had the first tractor home. But Willie got his nose in front for a while when he got his tractor and his power-drive binder home in one year.

Now you might have thought that a bit of good common sense would have been brought to the rivals' relationship when they took wives - but you'd have been wrong. Willie and Alexander expected their wives to be all that a wife should be and a new vehicle for their rivalry. There was the fur coat and the better fur coat, the car and the better car to be seen in going to church, the holiday at Stonehaven and the holiday at Strathpeffer, the formica fitted kitchen and the mahogany fitted kitchen.

And so it went on into old-age when Alexander conceived of his master-plan for an ultimate triumph. He went down to Inverurie and commissioned for himself the biggest gravestone they'd done since the last time one of the Forbes-Leiths had been in. It would dominate the little graveyard and would surely show up whatever little thingie his heirs would put up for poor Willie.

As luck would have it Alexander died first and sure enough Willie was dismayed when, a month after the funeral, he went back to the graveyard where the masons had placed his old rival's stone. What a challenge that was. It was more of a memorial than a gravestone. The mason had been told how big it had to be and that it had to be 'artistic' and good man that he was he had done his best. There it was, fifteen feet high and looking like no-one knew what, except the young schoolmaster who came from Edinburgh and said it looked like the Scott Monument in Princes

164

Street - but upside down. At any rate the village was impressed.

So was Willie but he was damned if he would be outdone. He hastened off to Aberdeen and commissioned himself a monument sixteen feet high and with Grecian urns on it.

It was a hellovan expense but there was never money better spent, or so it seemed, as Willie enjoyed a few happy months contemplating his final triumph which surely could not be long delayed.

His quiet enjoyment was quite upset though during the terrible gales in 1953 which blew down half the trees in Aberdeenshire. And didn't it also blow down Alexander's top-heavy artistic gravestone... or at least it would have if John Clark the haulage contractor had not seen it going. Wild night though it was, John managed to get a rope on the great granite monster just in time and by passing the rope round the telephone pole in the corner of the kirkyard and then hitching it to the back of his ten-ton tipper and drawing forward, he was able to get Alexander back more or less onto the plumb. He then tied the rope to the telephone pole in case another gust should threaten to blow it over again.

The storm having abated, Willie took his old bones out the next day to survey the damage of that terrible night. When he saw John Clark's work he took quite a turn and arrived back home in a grim mood.

"Aye Alice," he said to his wife, "I doubt Alexander's nae beat yet... the bugger's got the phone in next."

## CHAPTER FORTY

# A Trip to Smithfield

THERE'S NOTHING quite so engaging as a lad or a lass who arrives on a farm all bright-eyed and willing to work... and it's even better if they are able as well.

So it was with young Albert when he arrived at Moss-side of Drumglade. He wasn't especially well put-out: his jacket, which had been his big brother's, was just some big to be smart and it had certainly seen service, but his shoes shone and so did his face. And old Wattie Brown felt sure he'd got a right loon when, at yoking time next morning, he was waiting at the stable door with clean wellingtons. "Always a good sign that," Wattie thought to himself.

Wattie had managed the place since his father died twenty years ago. That had been a sad day in a way but it had left the way clear at last for Wattie and Lil. God knows they had waited long enough for their turn of the big bed in the front room at Mossie's croft. In fact they maybe left it too late - or maybe it was something that had happened to Wattie, for he had fought in the Kaiser's war, but at any rate they had no children.

That's often a particularly hard blow for farmers because they live by the reproduction of their animals and are used to regarding the infertile as useless, and culling them out ruthlessly.

But if Lil and Wattie felt their lack of issue, they never let on. They were made for one another really, for if Lil had a narrow outlook, that fitted perfectly into Wattie's lifestyle. She was able to marvel at his achievements at the mart, at the bargains he was able to pick up at the roups, and she shared the caring for and his love of the few animals at Moss-side of Drumglade.

The thirty acres of middling land supported them well enough, for their needs were few and their diligence great. They reared a dozen calves a year and sold them as medium stores at Drumglade market and they sold some eggs for cash. But mainly, the Brown's business was self-sufficiency. Between the yard and the field they grew their own fruit and vegetables, their ten acres of bog provided them with an inferior peat, they had hens to eat and for their eggs and their cow Doris provided milk and cheese as well as rearing the twelve calves, three at a time. At dinner-time Wattie shut the calves in the calf pen and after supper-time Lil went and milked Doris for the house and then let the calves back in for the leavings and what they could get till dinner-time next day.

The two had managed so long by themselves that it came as a surprise to the village when they took on that loon, though there were those who said it was because they had none of their own. But I have a different story.

Wattie had always wanted to go to London for the great Christmas fatstock show at Smithfield market. They could never have afforded it before the war of course, but thanks to Hitler and a bit of absent-minded bookkeeping, they'd been able to put past a tidy sum during the war off the hens. In fact, with the rationing, they were still paying right well even in 1947. And again, though Wattie could see nothing wrong with it really, he knew his egg trade was illegal so he'd kept it all under the bed and that was just a worry.

So what better way to solve that problem than to fulfil a life's ambition and go to Smithfield? But would the loon manage?

"Nae bother at aaa'," was the loon's verdict on that.

Would he mind to milk the coo? Meat the calves?"

"You be sure I'll manage," said Albert, or Bertie as they'd decided to call him.

Wattie was more or less reconciled to going when, on the very eve of the departure, Doris was struck down with milk fever.

167

Well that was it, they couldn't go now. No no, they would have to stay and maybe go to Smithfield Show next year.

But Bertie was quite adamant: "Awa ye go tae London. I'll easy look efter the coo and aaathing. My father eence had five coos wi milk fever and I cured them aa'."

Against his better judgement, Wattie took Lil to Smithfield and spent the most miserable few days of his life trailing round the show, and trailing round the sights of London, and trailing along Oxford Street, worrying himself sick about everything that would have gone wrong at the croft. What an idiot he'd been to leave everything to a 15-year-old loon - however confident and cheery he might have been.

And Lil hadn't that good a time either. The whole thing was right over her head. She had only once shown a real flash of excitement on the whole trip. It was when they went on the bus tour round the sights of London. Wattie had got them a seat right up at the front with the conductor who laid off continually:

"You are now passing St Paul's Cathedral," and "we're now entering 'orse guard parayde. And this ere's the faymous Picadilly Circus."

A big marmalade cat dashed across the road.

"Oh aye," said Lil, "and fa's cattie was that?"

Well well, to his great relief Wattie finally won home, in an agony of suspense. He was met in the close by the loon, with a cheery face and clean wellingtons.

"How did you get on Bertie?"

"Nae bother at aaa'," said the loon.

"You did athing I tell't ye?"

"Oh aye, and I've painted half the barn door."

Wattie could hardly bear to ask about his Doris, but the loon was so obviously in command:

"And how's ma coo?"

"Oh aye, she's deid," said the loon... cheerily.

# CHAPTER FORTY-ONE

# The Laird

"NO WONDER your father's having such bother making his estates pay. English lairds are all the same. No idea how to treat their tenants you see. Gave them nothing for centuries, kicked them around and kicked them out at will, whenever farming fashion and a fast pound suggested a change in estate management policy. Then charged all the rent the market would bear when times were hard and encouraged the tenants to take up the lives of gentlemen in good times, so that when the next slump came there wasn't a tenant on their estates who could remember what a good day's hard work felt like, or that it started before ten o'clock in the morning.

"No, no. The reason the Scottish lairds have survived to so much better an extent than the quality of our land or the left-wing tendencies, which are much stronger north of the Border, as you know, is that we have a greater sense of community. It all stems from the clan system. It's quite strong; very strong really, still in Scotland. It makes us care for our people. And in the old days they really were our people. Old Ranald there," pointing to an ancient progenitor hanging darkly from below the minstrel's gallery, "he was responsible for every man, woman and child in the six glens. And he was responsible too. If as much as a cow was stolen by a neighbour, Ranald used to sort it out or stand good the cow. And if a raiding party from across the hills were responsible, the old man would lead the reprisal raids. If a man was killed, the chief took care of the wife and children. You see, in Scotland being a laird was as much a duty as a right. You were the leader of the community but its servant as well, don't you know.

"And you know Richard, that clan spirit is still here... we all feel it. When my father raised his battalion in the six glens for the First World War, he had to turn away enough volunteers to form another battalion... well somebody had to stay and look after the damned estate. Just as well more didn't go really... I've still got the odd tenant I've got to house because they were widowed in that war. But that's just it. The people belong. We care about one and other so when a minor depression hits farming and you Englishmen have to sell the family silver or let out your Great Halls for those ghastly Medieval banquets, we just do what has to be done... share what there is and get by."

Lord Alexander was sharing not only all that wisdom but a bottle of twenty-five year old malt with his old school chum, the honourable Richard Elmtree. He always liked to have a pal for the last day of the grouse before the tenants' bang. He always kept one good drive back for the occasion and a few good bottles. It was all very well saying, as some did, that malts don't get much better after twelve years but Alexander knew that they got much better in one respect: "after they're twenty years old hardly anyone else can afford them."

It had been a great end to a very good season. Alexander and Richard had shot seventy-two brace between them and had only stopped because they had had enough. Not only that, but Alexander had had three left and rights on the trot and better still Richard, whose guns were up at the time, couldn't even pretend he hadn't seen them.

The last of the thousand-pound-a-day Belgians had left; they were nearly all coming back next year, and this year none of the cheques had bounced. Oh yes, things were going well and the laird was in expansive mood. The sort of mood unkind people might have called pompous. It was quite clear that Mr Elmtree wouldn't have to do much of the talking that night. And with a storm roaring up outside and the logs piled high in the great fireplace of the Great Hall, it was very hard to imagine a more

171

congenial place to be.

There was an interruption though. McGregor bustled in. I'm sorry to disturb you but Tigh Na Bulg is here. He's in a bit of a state and says he must see you.

With the sigh of one weighed down by the responsibilities of feudal protector, Alexander assented.

William MacAllan had on the good suit and was soon steaming as he stood between the laird and the fire, twisting his cap in his hand. He knew, of course, that the laird would have given him a small dram of his first-rate whisky if he hadn't had company and he wouldn't have come at all if things hadn't reached such a pass.

The farmhouse at Tigh Na Bulg needed a new roof - at least on the north face. The wife had been at him for months, and since he had mentioned it at the term, one of the timbers where the worst leak had been had actually broken, and that had shifted the whole side of the roof which was now leaking all over the place.

And here, with the worst of the winter still to come and the youngest bairn with that cough she'd had since harvest, and the wind in the north tonight and the wind being driven into the house, he just couldn't leave things any longer.

The laird took on a serious countenance which grew more

concerned in its appearance as the tale developed. Well now, Willie, I can see you're depressed and I'll overlook the fact that you've come in here with your troubles when I've got guests. The fact is Willie that, as I've explained to you before, this estate is a partnership between you, the tenants, and myself. In the good times we all make money and there is some available for improvements of the kind which you mention, and in bad times we have to struggle together, tighten our belts, cut corners, make do and mend. Now these are very difficult times, as you know. This capital gains business has cost my financial interests in the city a fortune, and with all these Belgians having been here since the twelfth, non-stop, there's a huge tax bill there again. So I'm afraid you'll just have to wait for the repairs to your roof till times improve... maybe before next winter.

Thank you M'Lord thank you. Well, well, well - if things are as bad as that, I suppose I'll just have to go back and tell the wife to move everything away as far as we can from that north wall, and I'll see what I can do with a tarpaulin in the morning. Goodnight, M'Lord... and goodnight to you too sir."

The two were left to get back to their dram. But for all that the guest was untutored in the benevolent ways of the Scottish aristocracy, the interview he had witnessed had left him somewhat uneasy. "Surely you were a bit hard on him," said the Honourable Richard Elmtree. "He seemed a decent enough chap to me".

"Silly beggar," said the laird, "If he'd just stuck in I'd have built him a new house, never mind repairing his roof. The old one is absolutely knackered you know."

CHAPTER FORTY-TWO

# From the classroom -
## Teacher's Pet

DESPITE HIS well-known talents for telling you in a flash how much the steel for a new portal-framed shed forty by one hundred by eighteen feet at the eaves will cost, Geordie the Blacksmith had been slow at the school. He wasn't so bad at the maths but at essays he was, not to put too fine a point upon it, rubbish. It may well be that his trouble was a lack of dedication as much as a lack of talent, but whatever the reason, the result was that Geordie hated the English teacher and she hated him.

Geordie Halley was the very opposite of the teacher's pet. She was forever holding the boy up to ridicule and making the most unfavourable, though perhaps not altogether unfair, comparisons between his work and that of his classmates, especially quines - and extra especially with Mary. She was Randall Pearson, the minister's, daughter and "awful good at essays".

Well now, on this occasion, Miss McWilliam announced that Primary Six would write an essay in class and that the subject would be 'The Flowers of Springtime'. Geordie's young heart sank as it had often sunk before. It wasn't that he didn't know anything about the flowers that bloom in the spring. He knew quite a lot. They were what his mother made him hoe out of her yard when the warmer weather came, and the flowers of spring were the things farmers sprayed their barley for, that they eliminated by sowing crystals along with the neep seeds and that the

174

roadmen were always spraying the roadsides to discourage. No, no. George knew all about weeds, it was just that he couldn't put his knowledge down on paper to suit 'Auld McWilliam'. The class would be another hour's boredom followed by another public humiliation.

But help was at hand. By good luck, of a kind that he had found in short supply in that class, Geordie was on this occasion sat right next to the champion essay writer, Mary Pearson. Now even then, and despite his inability at essays, George was a resourceful lad and with the desks being tightly packed in the little classroom, he was able to copy Mary's essay out, word for word.

"Right Halley, stand up boy and read your essay out to the class," said Miss McWilliam, emphasising the word essay in a way that would have sounded better if she'd called it a "so-called essay".

For once the young essayist was delighted. He had a good essay to read out for a change. Oh, the unaccustomed praise that would be coming his way. He read it out and sat down.

Sadly, the expected praise did not materialise:

"That's absolute rubbish, rubbish boy. Just your usual: you've nothing to say; you can't write; and thank goodness you read it out so I didn't have to see your dreadful spelling.

"Now Mary Pearson, will you read your essay out so the class can hear what an essay should be like," Miss McWilliam purred.

Poor Mary Pearson then had to get up and read out - word for word - the essay the teacher had just described as rubbish.

I'm afraid I can't finish that story properly by telling you what Miss McWilliam had to say about that. George got off with his copying all right, but when I asked him what the teacher had to say about it, all he would say was:

"What could she say?"

# The Last Word

MY SECOND classroom story involves a class of five-year-olds at Turriff in Aberdeenshire. It was after dinner-time and the teacher was trying to get her thirty charges to have a post-prandial nap, or at least to pretend. Her job though, which was always going to be an uphill struggle, was being sabotaged by the teacher in the next room who was having discipline problems. Those, she was trying to overcome by bellowing at her charges to "Sit down, shut up and behave," in a monstrous contralto.

A little voice piped up from one of the supposedly sleeping beauties:

"That wifie's got a big voice," it said.

"Now James, sleepies time. Doon yer heidie."

But James was not silenced for long;

"Oh Miss, that wifie's got an affa loud voice," he persisted, in a voice that was quite loud itself, and anything but sleepy.

"Shut up James, you little brat," said his teacher in a voice that gave promise that, in the right circumstances, she too could achieve a pretty impressive volume, "or I'll report you to Mr Shepherd and you'll not get out at playtime. Now put your head down and go to sleep."

That fairly put the head down and silence reigned in Primary One while the teacher next door continued to roar discipline into her charges.

After a minute or so of this, the voice piped up again for, despite the risks, James could not resist the last word;

"Aye, but she has, though," he said.

# General Knowledge

AND FINALLY: A class of country children of mixed age and ability were enduring a zoology lesson. They were being asked to identify pictures of animals round the class. The teacher held up a picture of a lion and asked what it was:

"A lion, Miss."

"Good, and what's this one William?"

"A tiger, Miss."
"Correct, and what's this?"
"A rhinoceros, Miss."

"Very good, Sandy, and what's this?" said the teacher
holding up a picture of a sheep.

Sandy shook his head.

James shook his head.

Alisdair shook his head too.

"Oh, for goodness sake," said the teacher. She turned to the
shepherd's son; "Tell them what this is Johnny," she said.

Johnny peered at the picture, scratched his head and wrung
his hands.

"Come along, boy," snapped the teacher, who suspected she
was being had.

"Well Miss, would it be a twa-shear Border-Leicester tup?"

# CHAPTER FORTY-THREE

# *Clochandichter*

THIS STORY is really about Scottish hospitality, or more especially about the way in which country folk press cups of tea,
scones and drams on the few visitors they have. And I saw a rare
example when I was over in Islay buying cattle in 1978. There
were two days of sales, when the islanders disposed of the calves
their cows had produced to be bought, mostly by farmers from the
mainland of Scotland and beyond, to be fattened for the butchers.
And the second day started at the farm of a most interesting
gentleman who had originated in England but had migrated to
Islay where he had become a most extensive farmer with many
enterprises, including a lobster farm. At any rate when we arrived
for the on-farm auction sale of several hundred suckled calves we
were ushered into the house to partake of the most indulgent feast
of sandwiches, cake and dainties as well as tea.

There must have been forty of us in the bright, warm farm
kitchen and the farmer's wife, a comfortable lady in her middle
age, clucked about her brood of cattle buyers, insisting with the
tarts and the tea.

One of the late arrivals was a dealer from the North-east.
And it was no wonder he wasn't first, for the previous night he
and a pal of his had been uproariously fu. I can vouch for that for
I was having a nightcap in the bar when the two heroes decided
that it was time to go to their beds, for they would need to be bright
and alert to buy their cattle the next morning at 9.30. At any rate,

to judge by the seriousness of their conversation and the unsteadiness of their posture, their thirsts must have been slaked.

Well now, it must have been just before one o' clock when they left the bar for bed, and all might have been well had they had a room on the ground floor - for it was the stairs that beat them. To cut a long story short it was just after two o' clock when they both made it together to the top of the stairs - each of them having made it on more than one occasion only to find that his mate was lying asleep half way up, or had fallen right down to the bottom again. Then he would have to go down to help his friend and that often proved a tricky business.

So after a night like that, Billy the cattle dealer could be forgiven for sleeping in. And when our hostess saw him she beamed, for as well as being a sociable fellow, he was a considerable buyer of cattle. "Oh Billy, you've come back to see us, come away in," and she offered and received a warm round hug. "Now Billy, will you have a cup of tea - or a dram?" "Oh, " said Billy slowly, "it's too early in the morning for tea." So the dram was duly poured and, in truth, we all had one.

The hospitality on that farm may have been particularly lavish, but it does seem to be a point of pride among farmers not to let people off the place without some form of sustenance. I had an old potato merchant friend who said he far preferred dealing south of the border. There he could see the potatoes, do his deal, pass the time of day and be off the farm in well under an hour. But in Scotland he had to put up with ages of additional haggling and endless hospitality. A week's business in England took him a month in Scotland as he slurped his way round the country on a tide of tea and drams. My potato friend was visiting a farm in Fife. It was a big farm with a lot of potatoes to sell; it was a foul day and by the time the crops had been walked he and his clerk were thoroughly soaked. "Now you'll just stay for lunch," said the farmer.

My friend agreed for he had been entertained there before and it would be a good lunch with a dram before it - just to bring in the thaw.

The hostess was charming. How nice that he was able to stay

and yes, there was plenty of beef and if she might be excused, she would go and put on some extra vegetables.

Then the farmer had a fine idea. His two guests would be the better of a bath and a change of underwear. So he took them upstairs, put the clerk in the bathroom and my friend in the farmer's private bathroom, after giving them a supply of dry underwear.

Now the private bathroom was one of those modern conveniences made from the prosperity the war and the post-war shortages had brought to British farmers. It had a door from the hall, of course, but my friend didn't know that the other door led to his hostess's bedroom - and did not think to lock it.

Now the lady of the house didn't know about the ablutions that were taking place and when she had nipped upstairs to see to her hair after putting on the extra potatoes and bulking up the stew with carrots and swede, she heard water running in her private bathroom and presumed it was her husband.

In she went to have words with him. As luck would have it, my friend was bending down in the shower to pick up the soap so that when she entered the farmer's wife was confronted with a large white posterior.

She gave it an almighty smack and said: "That'll teach you to bring in folk for lunch without telling me when there's hardly anything in the house. And I'm late for my bridge ladies." She stamped out without waiting for an answer, or for a second look.

Nothing was said at lunch but then after all, one well-fed middle aged backside does look much like another when it's bending down to pick up soap.

# Glossary

These words are Doric unless otherwise specified.

aa *all*
aboot *about*
ae *one*
aff *off*
affa *very*
airms *arms*
a mite American *much*
anither *another*
arles *small payment to seal a contract of employment*
ay, *yes,*
ay ay fit like *hallo how are you*
aye *always* or *ever*
ava *at all*
awa *away*
baain *baaing*
baillie *man who looks after cattle*
bantie *bantam often pronounced buntin*
bairns *children*
beddum hose *socks worn by the bride to the bridal bed*
bein *being*
Blue Toon *Peterhead. Home to the blue mogganers*
borra Glasgow *bother,* Nae borra *no trouble at all*
breered *emerged from the ground. Breer is the green sheen a newly emerged crop shows. Sc brairded*
breeks *trousers*
breem *broom*
breenge *lunge*
breid *oatcake*
brig *bridge*
butcher's pen *the animals which are not thought good enough for breeding end up in it*

182

| | |
|---|---|
| ca' | *fetch in* |
| ca'ed | *called* |
| caint | American *can't* |
| cairt | *cart* |
| callants | *young men* |
| casting | *selling as past their best for breeding* |
| canna | *can't* |
| clay cuttie | *clay pipe* |
| clochandichter | *the very last - usually  dram* |
| close | *farmyard*, Glasgow *common entrance to a tene ment* |
| coo | *cow* |
| coont | *count* |
| coorse | *cruel/ course* |
| coupit | *tipped over* |
| crawlin roon | *crawling round, crawling along* |
| cried, cryin | Glasgow *called, calling* |
| crop | *haircut* |
| cushie | *cushet dove or wood pigeon* |
| dae | *do* |
| deid | *dead* |
| deen | *done* |
| deein | *doing* |
| dinna, divn't, disna | *don't, doesn't* |
| doo | *dove, generic name for all pigeons, cushet doo, tame doo and ony ither doo* |
| dookin | *diving, bathing* |
| doon | *down* |
| doot | *doubt* |
| dour | *ill-humoured* |
| dunt | *bump* |
| dyke | *stone wall* |
| een, eence | *one, once* |
| efter | *after* |
| erses | *backsides* |
| fae | *from* |

| | |
|---|---|
| fairmies | *farms* |
| far | *where* |
| farra | Glasgow *father* |
| fase | *fetch* |
| fee, fee'd | noun *wage* verb *make a contract of employment.* |
| feart | *frightened* |
| fifty-sixer | *fifty-six pound weight* |
| fit | *what/how much* |
| fite | *white*, fite coo *white cow* |
| fleeced | *cheated out of all money* |
| float | *lorry for transporting livestock* |
| foo | *how* |
| fu | *drunk* |
| funcy | *fancy* |
| fushionless | *lacking energy or initiative* |
| gae'd | *went* |
| gairden | *garden* |
| garron | *Highland pony* |
| gaun | *going* |
| gey | *very* |
| gie, gie's | *give, give me. Gie's a hud o yer ex, give me the axe.* |
| ging | *go* |
| girnal | *storage chest* |
| girned | *grumbled* |
| goldarnit | American *meaningless slang exclamation* |
| graipe | *basic four-pronged tool for mucking byres, not to be mistaken for a fork which has two prongs and is best for moving straw* |
| greive | *foreman of farm workers. Not to be confused with the foreman who is the first tractorman* |
| grey lady | *Mr Ferguson's greatest tractor* |
| g'wa | *literally 'go away'. "come off it"* |
| guddle | *catch fish by hand* |
| gushet | *awkward bit you are left with in ploughing any but a square field.* |
| hae, haein | *have, having* |

| | |
|---|---|
| haff | Highland *have* |
| hairst | *harvest* |
| hale | *whole* |
| hame | *home* |
| haud | *hold* |
| heid | *head* |
| hey min | *impolite "excuse me"* |
| hinna | *have not* |
| hoosies | *houses. Childrens game...pretend housekeeping.* |
| hoi polloi | Greek *the many, the common people* |
| hud, huddin | on *hold, putting on plenty* |
| humphed | *carried with effort* |
| hunner | *hundred* |
| intil | *into* |
| jist | *just* |
| kebbuk | *farmhouse cheese* |
| kent | *knew* |
| kind | *sort of,* a kind of *a sort of* |
| kirkin | *going to church, wedding* |
| kirkyard | *churchyard* |
| kitchie-deem | *servant girl who works in the kitchen* |
| knackered | *done/exhausted* |
| kye | *cattle* |
| lames | *bits of broken china much prized to serve as the real thing in games of "hoosies"* |
| lang | *long* |
| larn | American *teach* |
| lead | *lift the sheaves from the stooks and leading them home to the cornyard to be built into rucks or thrashen.* |
| lift, tak the lift o | *make fun of* |
| likit | *liked* |
| limmer | *loose or disreputable woman* |
| loon | *boy* |
| lowse | *finish work.,* literally *unhitch the horses* |
| mair | *more* |
| mak | *make* |

185

| | |
|---|---|
| mannie | *man - derogatory, diminutive* |
| meat | *feed, food,* to meat the men *to feed the men* |
| menage a trois French *threesome* |
| min | *man* |
| miscry | *speak badly of* |
| mither | *mother* |
| mony | *many* |
| morn | *tomorrow* |
| mouser | *moustache* |
| na, nae | *no, no/not* |
| neen | *none* |
| neeps | *turnips* |
| neep-hasher | *machine for chopping turnips* |
| nicht | *night* |
| noo | *now* |
| oilies | *men who work for oil companies* |
| ontil | *onto* |
| ony | *any* |
| or | *until* |
| orraman | *general farm worker* |
| ower, ower muckle | *over/too, too much* |
| parkie | *a small field* |
| peching | *panting* |
| peesies | *lapwings* |
| ploo | *plough* |
| poinded | *seized by the bailiff* |
| providan | *dowry* |
| puckle | *small number* |
| pu, puin | *pull, pulling,* puin neeps, *pulling turnips out of the ground* |
| quarters | *volume of grain equal to eight bushels. Thus there are five quarters of good barley to the tonne and nearer four and a half quarters of first class wheat* |
| quine | *girl* |
| redd | *clear/empty* a redd-up *a mess* |
| richt | *right/proper* |

| | |
|---|---|
| rickle | *badly built* |
| rinnin | *running* |
| roaded | *on the move, started onto the road* |
| roup | *auction* |
| rouping | *selling at auction* |
| sair | *sore/very* I'm sair needin'/ a sair heid |
| sark | *shirt* |
| sax | *six* |
| shawed | *with shaws,* weel shawed *having developed good shaws* |
| shoogle | *shake something to work it into place* |
| sixsome | *a reel for six dancers* |
| smiddy | *blacksmith's workshop* |
| some | *too,* some mony *too many* |
| speared | *asked to stay on at end of contract* |
| starries | *starlings* |
| steam mill | broth for the steam mill *make enough broth for the 13 or so men who made up the squad on the steam mill at threshing time* |
| steel | *stool* |
| stingey | *mean* |
| stooking | *placing sheaves of grain upright in eights or tens* |
| stots | *castrated male cattle* |
| stovies | *dish of potatoes, onions and dripping* |
| strae | *straw* |
| straik | *if you go five times to the field for turnips you have completed five straik(pl)* |
| stucken | *stuck* |
| suppie | *small quantity* |
| swipin | *sweeping,* swipin the lum - *sweeping the chimney* |
| tae | *to* |
| teed | Highland *indeed* |
| tak | *take,* tak the lift of *make a fool of* |
| tapner | *hand tool for wresting neeps from the ground* |
| tatties | *potatoes* |
| tell't | *told* |

| | |
|---|---|
| than | *then* |
| thrawn | *obstinate* |
| threadin | *threading* |
| thrive | *be in vigorous health* |
| til | *to* |
| timmer | *wooden* |
| tinkie | *tinker* |
| toon | *town* |
| townser | *town dweller* |
| twa | *two* |
| twa-sheer | *2 year old shearling* |
| waal | *well* |
| waur | *worse* |
| weel | *well* |
| whar | *where* |
| whit, whit like | *what, what sort* |
| wi | *with* |
| wifie | *woman* |
| winna | *will not* |
| wir | *our* |
| wis | *was* |
| woa | *stop. instruction usually to a horse* |
| Yah | American *you.* Home Counties *yes* |
| ye, yer | *you, your* |
| yoking | verb *starting work* , noun *six till eleven or one till six* |
| zat | Glasgow *is that* |

# Also from Ardo Publishing

## *Green Heritage* by John R. Allan

*This novel was written in the early thirties and published posthumously in 1990. It is the story of a successful young London business man who discovers his roots in North-east Scotland.*
*Price £12.50*

## *A Lucky Chap* by Sir Maitland Mackie

*This is the autobiography of Sir Maitland, who with his father founded what became the biggest farming business in Scotland. It recalls his upbringing on the farm at Tarves. It also tells about his time as the Queen's representative in Aberdeenshire and how he got on with the Royals.*
*It tells mostly of eighty years of fun.*
*Price £12.50*

## *Cottar and Croft to Fermtoun* by Mary Michie

*The  autobiography of a Buchan quine who gave up her own ambitions to help her young man achieve his. They started married life as cottars, living in a tied house but by their own industry and that of their family, they achieved their goal of farming on their own behalf and ultimately of being owners of their own fermtoun. Mary remembers every detail.*
*Price £11.95*

## *Farmer's Diary* by Charlie Allan

*Charlie began writing the Farmers Diary column in the then Glasgow Herald in 1989 on his return to the family farm after a three year spell in Kenya. Each piece (nearly) was enhanced by a cartoon from Jim Turnbull and the column became a source of great enjoyment to farmers and non-farmers alike. The diary has been reproduced as a series of five volumes of which volume five is still to be published. It is planned for Christmas 1997.*

## *Volume I*

*This diary tells how Charlie got the farm going again, tried to keep the banker happy and re-established a place in the North-east community of Methlick. It covers a long year to Christmas 1990.*
*Price £12.50*

## *Volume II*

*Charlie continues his record of the constant battle with the weather and beaurocracy. He recounts the fun had by Mossie, Red Rooster and the other lads of the discussion group which meets at the Salmon Inn on a Sunday night to blow about crop yields or drown sorrows when the weather wins. This volume covers the year 1991 and continues to the end of February 1993.*
*Price now £9.95*

## *Volume III*

*Volume III covers the period from March 1992 to the end of June 1993. Charlie is still trying to grow the 4-tonne crop. There are marriages and births among the lads of the discussion group; sales and purchases of farms. But the biggest changes are brought in by the EC in the form of set-aside, and the EC commissioner from Ireland, Mr MacSharry, becomes the hero of Volume III.*
*Price £9.95*

## Volume IV

*Volume IV covers the period from June 1993 to mid October 1994. The Irishman enters the scene, buying one of Mossie's outfarms. He has new ideas for the Discussion Group to chew over and even has Mossie buying cattle. The 1994 harvest is a good one and Charlie may have made the four tonne crop,*
*Price £11.95*

All titles available at bookshops
throughout the North-east
or direct from Methlick
Please add £1 for postage

**Ardo Publishing Company Ltd.**
**Methlick, Aberdeenshire AB41 7HR**
**Tel/Fax 01651 806218**